THE DIVINE COMEDY: THE INFERNO

NOTES

including
- *Life and Background*
- *Dante's World*
- *The Figure of Virgil*
- *Structure of the* Comedy
- *Interpretation*
- *General Synopsis*
- *Summaries and Commentaries*
- *List of Characters*
- *Review Questions and Essay Topics*
- *Selected Bibliography*

by
Luisa Vergani, Ph.D.
University of San Diego
        College for Women

Cliffs Notes
INCORPORATED
LINCOLN, NEBRASKA 68501

Editor	Consulting Editor
Gary Carey, M.A. *University of Colorado*	*James L. Roberts, Ph.D.* *Department of English* *University of Nebraska*

ISBN 0-8220-0391-0
© Copyright 1969
by
Cliffs Notes, Inc.
All Rights Reserved
Printed in U.S.A.

1997 Printing

Cliffs Notes, Inc.   Lincoln, Nebraska

CONTENTS

CONTENTS

The Inferno Notes

LIFE AND BACKGROUND

Dante Alighieri was born in Florence in May, 1265, of an old family, of noble origin but no longer wealthy. His education was probably typical of any youth of his time and station: he studied the *trivium* and *quadrivium,* probably spent a year, or part of a year, at the University of Bologna, and came under the influence of some of the learned men of his day. Most notable of these was Ser Brunetto Latini, whose influence Dante records in his poem *(Inferno* 15).

In accordance with custom, Dante was betrothed in his youth to Gemma Donati, daughter of Manetto Donati. These betrothals and marriages were matters of family alliance, and Gemma's dowry was fixed as early as 1277, when Dante was twelve years old. There were at least three children: sons Pietro and Jacopo, and a daughter Antonia, who later entered a convent at Ravenna and took the name of Sister Beatrice. A third son, Giovanni, is sometimes mentioned.

There can be no doubt that the great love of Dante's life, and the greatest single influence on his work, was his beloved Beatrice. He first met her when he was nine years old and she was eight. The meeting took place in her father's home, probably at a May Day festival. Dante has described this meeting in his *Vita Nuova.* He tells of seeing the child Beatrice, wearing a crimson gown and looking like an angel. From that day on, his life and work was dedicated to her. He mentions no other meeting with her until nine years later, when he saw her on the street, dressed in white, accompanied by two other girls. She greeted him sweetly by name, and he was in raptures. A short time later, having heard gossip linking his name with another young woman, she passed him without speaking, and Dante mourned for days, determining to mend his ways.

If all this seems slightly preposterous, it is necessary to remember two things: that the young women of marriageable age were so strictly chaperoned that it was virtually impossible to have even a speaking acquaintance with them and that Dante's love for Beatrice was in the strictest tradition of courtly love, wherein the lover addressed his beloved as being completely out of his reach, and which viewed marriage between the lovers as impossible, in fact undesirable.

To what extent this was, at first, a true and lasting love cannot be determined. There is little doubt that Dante enjoyed the sweet misery of his situation and the sympathy of other ladies for his plight. After the death of Beatrice, and particularly after his exile, he put away his adolescent fancies, and Beatrice became a true inspiration.

Beatrice was married in about 1287 to Simone de' Bardi, a wealthy banker of Florence, a marriage of alliance of the two houses and one completely immaterial to Dante and his work.

Dante wrote many poems in praise of his lady during her lifetime, and when she died in 1290, at the age of twenty-five, he was inconsolable. He had had a dream of her death, and in her honor collected the poems he had written about her, which are included in the *Vita Nuova*. The later *Comedy* was also inspired by her memory.

Dante's public life began in 1289, when he fought against Arezzo at Campaldino. In 1295 he was one of the council for the election of priors of Florence, and in May, 1300, went as ambassador to San Gemignano to invite that commune to an assembly of the Guelph cities of Tuscany. From June 15 to August of the same year, he was one of the priors of Florence, and it was during that year that his best friend, Guido Cavalcanti *(Inferno,* Canto 22), caused a street riot on May Day. Guido was exiled to Sarzana by the officers of the city, one of whom was Dante. Sarzana proved so unhealthful that Guido petitioned to return to Florence, and was allowed to do so. He died of malaria, contracted in Sarzana, in August, 1300.

Dante was vigorously opposed to the interference of the pope in secular affairs, and was induced to take a stand with the Whites when the Blacks favored the intrigues of the pope. Charles of Valois was coming to Florence, ostensibly as a peacemaker between the two factions but in reality as a partisan of the Blacks and supporter of the pope. In October, 1301, Dante and two other men were chosen as ambassadors on a mission to Rome, rightly suspecting the motives of Charles as peacemaker. After they had left Florence, the Blacks easily took over control of the city with the help of Charles, and Dante was exiled from his native city, never to return.

The terms of exile were harsh: Dante was charged with graft, with intrigue against the peace of the city, and with hostility against the pope, among other things. The list of charges is so long that it is reminiscent of those brought against the political enemies of any party in power today. In addition, a heavy fine was imposed, and Dante was forbidden to hold public office in Florence for the rest of his life.

Dante did not appear to answer the charges—it probably would not have been safe to do so—and a heavier penalty was imposed: in addition to confiscation of his property, he was sentenced to be burnt alive if caught. Also, his sons, when they reached their legal majority at age fourteen, were compelled to join him in exile.

Thus began Dante's wanderings. At first he joined in the political intrigues of his fellow exiles, but, disgusted by what he considered their wickedness and stupidity, he formed a party by himself. It is not known exactly where he spent the years of his exile, though part of the time he was with the Malaspini, and he also spent time at the court of Can Grande della Scala in Verona, with whom he remained on good terms for the rest of his life.

Once during the years of his banishment his hopes for peace in Italy, and his own return to Florence, were revived. This was in the reign of Henry VII of Luxemburg, who announced his intention of coming to Italy to be crowned. Dante addressed a letter to his fellow citizens urging them to welcome Henry as emperor. When Henry was met by strong opposition, Dante in great bitterness sent a letter to him, urging him to put down the rebellion quickly; he also addressed a letter in similar vein to Florence, using abusive terms which could not be forgiven. When Henry's expedition failed, and the hopes of empire died with him, Dante was not included in the amnesty granted certain exiles. Later, amnesty was extended to him on the condition that he admit his guilt and ask forgiveness publicly, which the poet refused to do. His sentence of death was renewed.

Dante's last years were spent in Ravenna, under the protection of Guido Novello da Polenta. They seem to have been years of relative contentment in compatible company—but Ravenna was not Florence. One final mission was entrusted to Dante: he was sent to Venice in the summer of 1321 by his patron in an unsuccessful attempt to avert a war between Ravenna and Venice. On his return trip, he fell ill, possibly of malaria. He reached Ravenna and died there on the night of September 13, 1321.

He was buried with the honors due him. Several times during the following centuries, the city of Florence sought to have his body interred with honor in the place of his birth, but even the intercession of popes could not bring this about. His opinion of the citizens of his city was clearly stated in the full title of his great work: *The Comedy of Dante Alighieri, Florentine by Citizenship, Not by Morals.*

Dante still lies in the monastery of the Franciscan friars in Ravenna.

DANTE'S WORLD

Dante's world was threefold: the world of politics, the world of theology, and the world of learning. His *Comedy* encompasses and builds upon all of these, and so interdependent were they that it would be impossible to say that any one was the most important.

Throughout the Middle Ages, politics was dominated by the struggle between the two greatest powers of that age: the papacy and the empire. Each believed itself to be of divine origin and to be indispensable to the welfare of mankind. The cause of this struggle was the papal claim to temporal power, supported and justified by the spurious "Donation of Constantine." This document, which was a forgery of the eighth century, maintained that Emperor Constantine, before leaving for Byzantium, had transferred to the Bishop of Rome, Pope Sylvester I, political dominion over Italy and the western empire.

Dante lived in an era of virtually autonomous communes, ruled by either an autocratic hereditary count or a council elected from an aristocratic — and exclusive — few. The political situation was never stable, and the vendettas went on forever, family against family, party against party, city against city.

The strife began in the tenth century with Otto I, the emperor who laid the foundation for the power which was to transform Germany into the mightiest state in Europe and who dreamed of restoring the Holy Roman Empire. At the beginning of the eleventh century, the situation worsened, with Henry IV humiliated at Canossa by an aggressive opponent, autocratic Pope Gregory VII (Hildebrand).

In the first part of the thirteenth century, the growing conflict was headed by two outstanding antagonists: Innocent III, the most powerful of all the popes, and the brilliant Frederick II, King of Germany, Emperor of Rome, and King of Naples and Sicily, the most gifted of all the monarchs of the Middle Ages. The enmity of the pope, who was firmly resolved to free Italy from German authority, shook the stability of the empire, which was already undermined by the insubordination of the princes in Germany and the rebellion of some of the city-states of northern Italy.

When Frederick died in 1250, he left a very unstable situation to be handled by his successors, especially in Italy. There, in 1266, his illegitimate son Manfred was defeated and killed in the battle fought at Benevento against Charles of Anjou, who had been summoned to Italy by the pope. Two years later, this same Charles defeated Corradino, Frederick's grandson, at Tagliacozzo, and put him to death. Thus the line of the descendants of the great emperor was extinguished and Italy was lost to the empire.

In reading Dante, indeed throughout medieval history, one hears much about two major political factions, the Guelphs and the Ghibellines. In Italy the party lines were originally drawn over the dispute between the papacy and the emperor for temporal authority. The Ghibellines, representing the feudal aristocracy, wished to retain the power of the emperor in Italy as well as in Germany. The Guelphs were mainly supported by the rising middle-class merchant society, who hoped to rid Italy of foreign influence and maintain the control of governments in their independent communes. They espoused the cause of the papacy in opposition to the emperor.

The rivalry between the two parties not only set one city against another but also divided the same city and the same family into factions. In time the original alliances and allegiances became confused in strange ways. For example, Dante, who was a Guelph, was a passionate supporter of imperial authority all his life.

In Florence the Guelphs and Ghibellines succeeded each other, alternately ruling the city. During the rein of Frederick II, the Ghibellines, supported by the emperor, gained the upper hand and drove the Guelphs out of the city. But at the death of Frederick II, in 1250, the Guelphs were recalled to Florence for a temporary reconciliation and later gained control of the city.

The Ghibellines again returned to power in 1260, and ruled the city until 1266, but the next year the Guelphs, aided by French forces, gained supremacy in the city, and the Ghibellines left Florence, never to return.

Dante was an ardent White Guelph, putting his hopes for Italy's future in the restoration of the empire, and to the end of his days was politically active, though ultimately he was forced by the violence of his views to form a party "by himself," and, as a White, was actually allied to the Ghibellines.

Not even the supremacy of the Guelphs, however, endowed Florence with a peaceful and stable government, for in 1300 the Guelph party split into two factions: the Whites and the Blacks, led respectively by the families of the Cerchi and the Donati. The basis of this split was the usual blood-feud between two families. In nearby Pistoia, a family quarrel existed between two branches of the Cancelliere family. The first wife of the original Cancelliere was named Bianca, and her descendants called themselves Whites in her honor. The name of the second wife is not known, but her descendants, in opposition to the Whites, called themselves Blacks. The quarrel erupted into open violence after a murder committed by one Foccaccia (mentioned by Dante in Canto 32 of the *Inferno*).

The Guelphs of Florence, in the interests of maintaining the precarious peace of the district, intervened in the hostilities, and in so doing furthered the jealous rivalry of the Cerchi and the Donati families, who naturally took opposite sides. The city was torn by strife; personal ambitions, feuds, and the arrogance of individuals and families further agitated the situation.

At this point, the Blacks secretly enlisted the aid of Pope Boniface VIII, who intervened in the affairs of the city, largely in his own interest. The pope considered the throne of the empire still vacant, since Albert I had not received his crown in Rome. In his assumed capacity as vicar of the emperor, Boniface plotted to extend the rule of the church over the territory of Tuscany. To accomplish this, he first obtained the favor of the Blacks, then dispatched Charles of Valois, brother of the King of France, to Florence, ostensibly as a peacemaker, but actually as a supporter of the Blacks. In 1302, with the help of Charles of Valois, the Blacks gained control of the city. In the list of some six hundred Whites banished from Florence was the name of the citizen Dante Alighieri.

While the rest of Italy, like Florence, was troubled by rivalries between parties, or by wars of city against city, in Germany the emperor's throne was vacant, first because of an interregnum, then because of a conflict between two rival claimants. The emperor's position was still regarded as vacant by the Italians when the two emperors who followed, Rudolph of Hapsburg and Albert I, failed to come to Italy to be crowned and paid no attention to Italian affairs. Therefore when the news came that Henry of Luxemburg, who succeeded Albert I in 1308, was coming to Italy to oppose King Robert of Sicily, many Italians, for whom Dante was the most eloquent and fervent spokesman, welcomed the prospect with feverish enthusiasm. They saw in the figure of Henry the end of all the woes which had wracked the peninsula.

Henry was crowned at Milan early in 1311. Very soon after, he faced the armed hostility of the opposing party, which had Florence as its leader. Henry, nevertheless, was able to reach Rome and be crowned there in 1312. The coronation took place in the church of St. John Lateran rather than in St. Peter's because the latter was being held by the forces of King Robert of Sicily. The emperor was still fighting to unite the empire when he died in the summer of 1313, succumbing to a fever with suspicious suddenness. The death of Henry put an end forever to the expectations of Dante and all other Italians who had longed for the restoration of the imperial power in Italy.

Dante's theological ideas were strictly orthodox, that is, those of medieval Catholicism. He accepted church dogma without reservation. His best authorities for insight into the more complex problems confronting the medieval thinkers were Augustine, Albertus Magnus, and Thomas Aquinas. He followed the Pauline doctrine of predestination and grace as presented by Augustine, but he managed to bring this into a kind of conformity with free will, to which he firmly adhered. Man has inherited sin and death through Adam's fall, but also hope of salvation through Christ's redemption. God in his love created humans with the power of perceiving good and evil and the opportunity of choosing. On the basis of their choice depended their eternal bliss or damnation. Those who set their will against the divine law were sentenced to Inferno and everlasting torment. Those who sinned but confessed and repented were given their reward in heaven after a period of purifying atonement in Purgatory. Thus repentance, the acceptance of divine law, was the crux of judgment in the afterlife.

Among the familiar tenets of medieval theology, we recognize such concepts as the "seven deadly sins" in Purgatory and the corresponding seven virtues in Paradise. The doctrine that only those persons who had been baptized as worshipers of Christ were to be admitted to Paradise is expressed in the treatment of the souls in Limbo (*Inferno* 4). Of the many more complex theological concepts expounded through the *Commedia,* explanations will be offered in the textual commentaries.

In castigating the individual popes (and particularly his bitter enemy, Boniface VIII), he was in no way showing disrespect for the *office* of the papacy, for which he held the greatest reverence. He was, in fact, following the long tradition of critics, many of them in high places in the church, who had not hesitated to recall popes to the duties and responsibilities of the chair of Peter. Dante held to the ideal of the papacy and the empire as the dual guardians of the welfare of man, spiritual and secular, each deriving its separate powers directly from God.

Readers cannot fail to recognize Dante's erudition. He appears to have taken all learning for his province, or what passed for learning then. The fact that much of the scientific teaching was hopelessly in error is not Dante's responsibility. The fact that he displayed extraordinary curiosity and avid interest in all branches of scientific learning (geography, geology, astronomy, astrology, natural history, and optics) reveals something important about the poet's mind.

Among the concepts that influenced the plan of the *Commedia* was the belief that only the northern hemisphere of the earth was inhabited, that the southern hemisphere was covered with water except for the mount of Purgatory. The scheme of the heavens was dictated by the Ptolemaic, or geocentric, system of astronomy, upon which Dante based the entire plan of *Paradiso*.

THE FIGURE OF VIRGIL

In the Middle Ages, Virgil had come to be regarded as a sage and necromancer. Virgil's poems were used in the type of divination called *sortes,* in which the book is opened at random and a verse selected in the same manner, as an answer to a problem or question. The Bible has been, and still is, used in the same manner.

Virgil's *Aeneid* offered the pattern for the structure of Dante's Hell, but this alone is not the reason why Virgil was chosen as the guide through Hell. Dante himself salutes Virgil as his master and the inspiration for his poetic style; further, Virgil is revered by Dante as the poet of the Roman Empire, since his *Aeneid* tells the story of the empire's founding. Finally, in his fourth eclogue, Virgil writes symbolically of the coming of a Wonder Child who will bring the Golden Age to the world, and in the Middle Ages this was interpreted as being prophetic of the coming of Christ. Thus, in the figure of Virgil, Dante found symbolically represented the two institutions, church and empire, destined by God to save mankind.

STRUCTURE OF THE "COMEDY"

Dante lived in a world that believed in mystical correspondences, in which numbers—like stars, stones, and even the events of history—had a mystical significance. In planning the structure of the *Divine Comedy,* therefore, Dante had in mind a series of symbolic numbers: three, a symbol of the Holy Trinity; nine, three times three; thirty-three, a multiple of three; seven, the days of creation; ten, considered during the Middle Ages a symbol of perfection; and one hundred, the multiple of ten.

The plan was carried out with consummate precision. We find three *cantiche,* each formed by thirty-three cantos, totaling ninety-nine. The introductory first canto of the *Inferno* makes one hundred cantos in all. The entire poem is written in the difficult *terza rima,* a verse form of three-line stanzas, or tercets. The first and third lines rhyme, and the second line rhymes with the beginning line of the next stanza—again, three, and three.

Hell is divided into nine circles (in three divisions), the vestibule making the tenth; Purgatory is separated into nine levels, the terrestrial paradise making ten; and Paradise is formed by nine heavens, plus the Empyrean. The celestial hierarchies are nine and are divided into triads. The sinners in Hell are arranged according to three capital vices: incontinence, violence, and fraud. The distribution of the penitents in Purgatory is based on the threefold nature of their rational love. The partition of the blessed in Paradise is made according to the secular, active, or contemplative nature of their love for God. The very fact that each *cantica* ends with the word "stars" helps to demonstrate the studied plan of the whole work.

Inferno is a huge, funnel-shaped pit located with its center beneath Jerusalem, its regions arranged in a series of circular stairsteps, or terraces, diminishing in circumference as they descend. Each of the nine regions is designated for a particular sin, and the order of the sins is according to their wickedness, the lightest near the top of the pit and the most heinous at the bottom.

The punishments in Inferno are regulated by the law of retribution; therefore, they correspond to the sins either by analogy or by antithesis. Thus, for example, the carnal sinners, who abandoned themselves to the tempests of passion, are tossed about incessantly by a fierce storm. The violent, who were bloodthirsty and vicious during their lives, are drowned in a river of blood. The sowers of dissension, who promoted social and domestic separations, are wounded and mutilated according to the nature of their crimes.

INTERPRETATION

The *Divine Comedy* has had many interpreters. Some have followed Dante's own thought, as outlined so clearly in his letter to Can Grande; others appear to ignore it.

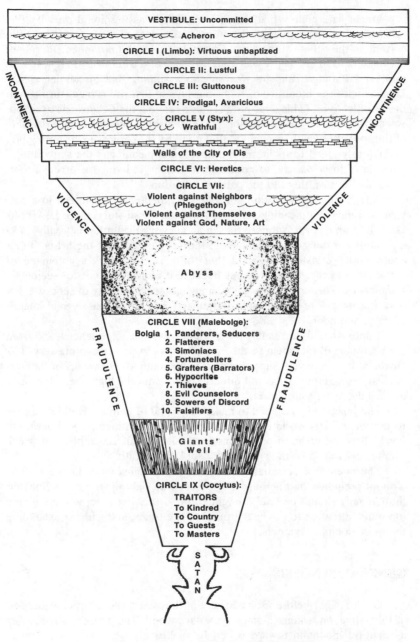

PLAN OF DANTE'S INFERNO

Dante said plainly that the first meaning was the literal one. By this he meant that the cantos tell the story of the state of souls after death, according to the beliefs of medieval Christianity. He did *not* mean, nor intend his readers to infer, that it was a literal story of a trip through Hell, Purgatory, and Paradise; and he was safe in assuming that his audience was familiar with the literature of such journeys, a favorite subject throughout the Middle Ages. (This does not preclude reading the *Comedy* as excellent science fiction.) Hell (or Purgatory, or Paradise) is, therefore, the *condition* of the soul after death, brought to that point by the choices made during life.

Closely allied to its literal and allegorical meaning is the stated moral purpose of the *Comedy:* to point out to those yet living the error of their ways, and to turn them to the path of salvation.

Allegory is, by definition, an extended metaphor, organized in a pattern, and having a meaning separate from the literal story. C. S. Lewis has said "It is an error to suppose that in an allegory the author is 'really' talking about the thing that symbolizes; the very essence of the art is to talk about both." Aristotle believed that for a poet to have a command of metaphor was the mark of genius because it indicated a gift for seeing resemblances. This implies the gift of imagination, the ability to set down not only the images of vision, but, particularly in Dante's case, vivid images of noise and odor.

Dante wanted his reader to experience what he experienced, and from the beginning of the poem to the end he grows in power and mastery. His language is deceptively simple and so is his method. He writes in the vernacular, using all its force and directness; it is not the high poetic language of tragedy, as he said himself.

The imagery is designed to make the world of Dante's Hell intelligible to the reader. His world is the world of the thirteenth-century church, but his Hell is the creation of his mind, an allegory of redemption in which Dante seeks to show the state of the soul after death.

The poem is a demanding one. The reader must enter Dante's world without prejudice, and perhaps T. S. Eliot was right in recommending that the *Comedy* should be read straight through the first time, without giving too much attention to the background of the times, and without examining the more complex symbols.

GENERAL SYNOPSIS

On the night before Good Friday in the year 1300, Dante, at the age of thirty-five, finds himself astray in a dark wood. The morning sun reveals a beautiful mountain toward which he makes his way, but his ascent is checked by three beasts: a leopard, a lion, and a she-wolf. Dante, therefore, is forced to return to the forest, where he is met by the shadow of Virgil, who promises to rescue him and take him on a journey through Hell, Purgatory, and Paradise (Canto 1). In undertaking the journey, Dante is troubled by fear; however, this is overcome when Virgil explains that he has been sent to his aid by Beatrice, who descended into Limbo to ask for his help. Moreover, Beatrice was sent by the Virgin Mary through her messenger, St. Lucia. Comforted by this, Dante follows Virgil as his guide and master (Canto 2).

After reading the dreadful inscription written on the gate of Hell, the two poets pass into the Vestibule where the uncommitted are tormented and then reach the bank of the river Acheron. Here the lost souls wait their turn to be carried across the river by Charon, an ancient boatman with flaming eyes who agrees only reluctantly to take Dante on his boat (Canto 3). In Limbo, the first circle of Hell, Dante is received by the great poets of the ages, Homer, Horace, Ovid, and Lucan. In the Palace of Wisdom he is also privileged to see the sages of antiquity, whose only punishment is being deprived of the vision of God (Canto 4).

Then Dante and Virgil enter Hell proper, which may be said to begin with the second circle. There the hideous Minos is seated as a judge, and the carnal sinners are tossed about by an incessant storm. The poets meet Paolo and Francesca and listen to their story of love and death (Canto 5). Among the gluttonous, guarded by the monster Cerberus and buried in mud in the third circle, Dante recognizes the Florentine Ciacco and receives from him a gloomy political prophecy. Then, as they talk about the resurrection of the body, Dante and Virgil move to the fourth circle (Canto 6), where Plutus reigns over the nameless mass of the prodigals and the avaricious, condemned to roll heavy stones against one another. This sight gives occasion for a disquisition upon Fortune. When Dante's doubts have been resolved, the two poets reach the fifth circle, the marsh of Styx, where the souls of the wrathful and sullen are condemned (Canto 7). The Florentine Filippo Argenti, one of the wrathful, tries to overturn the boat on which Dante is carried by the demon Phlegyas, but to Dante's satisfaction, Argenti is ferociously attacked by his companions.

Meanwhile Dante and Virgil come under the walls of the City of Dis, the sixth circle, to which, however, the fallen angels deny access (Canto 8). This is obtained only with the help of a heavenly messenger. Inside the City of Dis, the poets see the burning tombs in which the heretics are confined (Canto 9). Dante stops to speak with a great enemy, the Ghibelline Farinata degli Uberti, and also meets Cavalcante dei Cavalcanti, the father of his friend Guido (Canto 10).

When the poets approach the seventh circle, the air becomes so fetid that they have to halt for a while behind a tomb. While waiting to grow accustomed to the stench, they take advantage of the pause to discuss the division of the lower part of Hell (Canto 11). Finally the poets begin to descend through a deep valley and first meet the monstrous Minotaur, then reach a river of boiling blood, the Phlegethon, which forms the first section of the seventh circle. Here are plunged those violent against their neighbors, tyrants, and warmakers like Attila and Alexander the Great, watched over by the centaurs (Canto 12).

After being carried across the river by the centaur Nessus, Dante and Virgil enter the second round of the seventh circle, where the souls of the suicides grow like plants in a dreadful wood ruled by the hideous harpies. One of these plants is the soul of Pier delle Vigne, who narrates his sad story. In the same wood the reckless squanderers are seen by the poets being chased and torn to pieces by hounds (Canto 13).

The third round is formed by a desert of burning sand on which the blasphemers, sodomites, and usurers are exposed to a rain of fire. Among the blasphemers, Dante recognizes Capaneus (Canto 14); among the sodomites he encounters his master Brunetto Latini (Canto 15) and listens to the considerations of some famous men of ancient Florence in regard to the sad state of their city (Canto 16).

Then, after a contemptuous exchange with the usurers, Dante and his guide fly down to Malebolge, the eighth circle, on the back of the huge and repugnant monster, Geryon (Canto 17). Malebolge is the circle where the sinners of simple fraud are condemned. In the first bolgia the poets see the panderers and seducers, beaten with lashes; in the second the flatterers, plunged in a canal of excrement (Canto 18). In the third the simoniacs are sunk upside down in round holes, and from each hole protrudes a pair of feet with the soles ablaze. Dante approaches Pope Nicholas III and speaks to him (Canto 19). Then he reaches the fourth bolgia and, standing on the bridge overlooking it, watches the fortunetellers and the diviners who pace slowly and weep silently with their heads reversed on their bodies, so that they are obliged to walk backward (Canto 20).

Thence Dante and Virgil pass to the bridge overlooking the fifth bolgia, where the grafters are plunged into boiling pitch and tormented by black devils. The poets arrive just in time to see a senator of Lucca thrown into the pitch and torn to pieces by the hooks of the demons. At this point, since the bridge across the sixth bolgia lies broken, they have to seek help from the demons, and from their leader, Malacoda, obtain an escort to the next bridge (Canto 21). Walking along the bank of the canal, Dante and Virgil see the sinners lying in the pitch. One is hooked by the demons and pulled out to speak briefly with the poets. The unidentified Navarrese, after furnishing some information to the travelers, plays a trick on the demons who claw him. He escapes into the pitch, and the trick is immediately followed by a brawl in which the black creatures fall into the pitch themselves. The two poets take advantage of the incident and escape from the dangerous company (Canto 22).

After their flight, Dante and Virgil find themselves at the bottom of the sixth bolgia, where the hypocrites are punished by walking slowly and wearing heavy leaden friars' robes. At a certain point of their walk, the sinners step upon Caiaphas crucified on the ground. Two Jovial Friars talk to the poets and show them the way to climb to the seventh bolgia (Canto 23). This appears as a pit full of monstrous snakes and of naked men rushing in terror among them. They are the thieves. One of them, Vanni Fucci, relates to Dante a political prophecy (Canto 24); then the poet recognizes five noble Florentines and witnesses their endless and painful transformation from men into reptiles and vice versa (Canto 25).

Afterward, while addressing a lament to Florence, which has so many representatives in Hell, Dante reaches the bridge overlooking the eighth bolgia. The valley twinkles with innumerable little flames which conceal the souls of the evil counselors. One of them, Ulysses, gives Dante an account of his last journey and of his death (Canto 26) and another, Guido, Count of Montefeltro, inquires about the state of Romagna, and tells the story of his life (Canto 27).

When the poets come to the ninth bolgia they see a mass of bodies horribly mutilated. They are sowers of religious, political, and family discord, and are mutilated in different degrees. Pier da Medicina, Mosca dei Lamberti, and Bertrand de Born ask to be remembered in this world (Canto 28).

Dante would like to linger, hoping to see one of his kinsmen, Geri del Bello, but Virgil hurries him to the tenth bolgia, where the falsifiers are punished, all afflicted with horrible plagues and diseases. They are divided into four classes. Two of the alchemists, Griffolino d'Arezzo and Capocchio, speak to Dante (Canto 29). Later, Gianni Schicchi and Myrrha are identified among the evil impersonators, and Master Adam among the counterfeiters. Dante then watches a fight between Master Adam and Simon the Greek who belongs to the fourth class of sinners, the falsifiers of words, but being too attentive to the scene, is reproached by Virgil (Canto 30) and moves toward the ninth circle, the prison of traitors.

The ninth circle is a well, the bottom of which is a great frozen lake, Cocytus, formed by the infernal rivers that are draining there. Through the dusk it seems to Dante that he discerns the great towers of a city, but as he approaches them, he discovers that they are giants and Titans visible from the waist up. A giant, Antaeus, takes the travelers in his palm and places them on the ice at the bottom of the well (Canto 31). The traitors who are punished here are confined in four concentric rounds. In the first round (Caina) are the traitors to kindred, fixed in the ice except for their heads. Dante speaks to Camicion dei Pazzi, who identifies, among the others, Alessandro and Napoleone degli Alberti. In the second round (Antenora) are the traitors to country. Here Dante kicks Bocca degli Abati in the face and treats him savagely, then comes upon a sinner gnawing another traitor's skull and asks him to explain the reason why he is acting in such a bestial manner (Canto 32). The sinner, who is Count Ugolino della Gherardesca, answers that the head he is gnawing is that of Archbishop Ruggieri and tells Dante how he and his sons died of starvation. Then Dante visits the third round (Ptolomea), where are the traitors to friends and guests, among whom he meets Friar Alberigo and Branca d'Oria (Canto 33). Finally the poets reach Judecca, the fourth round, where the traitors to their masters and benefactors are completely covered with ice. In the center of the round they see Lucifer, who has three faces and is crushing Judas, Brutus, and Cassius in his three mouths. They climb down the thick hair of the demon's side, pass by the center of gravity and, through a natural dark passage, ascend once more to the upper world before daybreak on the morning of Easter Sunday (Canto 34), look up, and see the stars.

SUMMARIES AND COMMENTARIES

CANTO 1

Summary

At the midpoint of his life, Dante finds himself in a dark wood where there is no path. It is a fearful place, impenetrable and wild. Dante is unable to recall how he got here, and knows only that he has wandered from the path he should be following. He goes along the dismal valley of the wood to the foot of a hill, looks up, and to his joy sees the sun shining on the hilltop. The fears of the night are ended, and he looks back at the valley which no one leaves alive.

Dante rests for a time, then begins to climb the hill. He has barely started when he is confronted by a leopard, which blocks his path. Dante turns this way and that to evade it. This beast has not particularly frightened Dante, but it is soon joined by a hungry lion, more fearful in its aspect, and then by a she-wolf, which so terrifies Dante that he gives up the attempt to climb the hill. The she-wolf drives him back down into the darkness of the valley.

As Dante rushes headlong to escape the beast, a figure appears before him. It has difficulty in speaking, as though it had not spoken for a long time. Dante implores its help, whether it is spirit or man. The reply is given: it is the spirit of a man born in Mantua. He was born late in the reign of Julius Caesar and lived in the time of Augustus; he was a poet and wrote of Aeneas, son of Anchises of Troy. The shade asks why Dante has come back to this dark valley and why he did not continue his climb up the sunlit mountain.

Dante of course recognizes that this is Virgil, and hailing him as his master and his inspiration, points out the she-wolf which has driven him back. Virgil tells him that he must go another way, for this beast will not allow men to pass. She snares and kills them, and is so greedy she is never filled, but is always ravenous. Many are the animals with which she mates, but one day a hound will come that will cause her painful death. Virgil prophesies that this greyhound, whose food is wisdom, love, and courage, will come from the nation "between Feltro and Feltro," and will save Italy, chasing the she-wolf back to Hell.

Virgil commands Dante to follow him and see the harrowing sights of the damned, the hope of those doing penance, and, if he so desires, the realm of the blessed. Another guide will take him to this last realm, which Virgil may not enter.

Dante eagerly consents, and the two poets begin their long journey.

Commentary

Without preliminaries, Dante plunges into the story of his journey to salvation. He stands at the midpoint of his life — half the biblical three score and ten — and has lost his way: "I came to myself . . . ," he says — I found myself — I came to my senses. He has strayed from the true faith without realizing it, not knowing exactly how it came about, and is seeking to return. Through the allegory, he is saying that human reason can guide him back to faith — up to a point.

When Dante speaks of having strayed from the right path the reader should not assume that Dante has committed any specific sin or crime. Throughout the poem Dante is advocating that man must *consciously* strive for righteousness and morality. Man can often become so involved with the day-to-day affairs of living that he will gradually relapse into a sort of lethargy in which he strays from the very strict paths of morality.

For Dante, man must always be aware intellectually of his own need to perform the righteous act. Sin, therefore, is a perversion of the intellect. When Dante says he has strayed and that he does not know how he came to such a position, it simply means that by gradual degrees he has lapsed into a type of indifference and now this must be corrected. Thus the dark wood typifies a human life where every waking moment is not consciously devoted to morality.

Virgil stands for human reason, upon which Dante must depend for his return to grace, and explains that he was sent by another (Beatrice, symbolizing Revelation), though he does not name her until later. The figure of Virgil is not merely that of guide and master. In Dante's time Virgil was viewed as a "white magician," as his prophecy of the grey-hound shows, and in the *Inferno,* he uses formal incantations to command the spirits and demons of Hell. In later cantos he becomes a superhuman figure, fearing nothing.

A typically Dantean touch is the hoarseness of Virgil; it may be interpreted in several ways: that Virgil was not much read in Dante's time; that he has not spoken to a mortal since he was first conjured to make a descent into Hell, a journey he tells Dante about in Canto 9; or, what is most likely, that, as the voice of the empire, he has not been heard or heeded for a very long time. Note also that Virgil's spirit cannot speak until it is spoken to: a widely held belief in Dante's superstitious age, and one used by Shakespeare in *Hamlet.*

The three beasts, referred to in Jeremiah 5:6, are sometimes considered to have a double symbolism. Allegorically, the leopard is worldly pleasure, politically it is the city of Florence, so given to worldly pursuits; the lion is ambition, politically the royal house of France, which sought to rule Italy; finally, the she-wolf symbolizes avarice, and politically is the papacy, which Dante viewed as an avaricious religious entity seeking more and more secular power. There are, of course, many other interpretations, among them that the beasts symbolize lechery, pride, and covetousness; or the sins of incontinence, violence, and fraud, which are punished in the three divisions of Hell. Whatever they are, they stand firmly in the way of Dante's salvation.

The hound referred to has been the subject of controversy, but by some commentators has been taken to refer to Dante's friend and protector, Can Grande della Scala, the great Ghibelline leader. (Note: Can Grande means "great dog" in Italian.) His "nation" — the land where he ruled — was between Feltre and Montefeltro; Dante believed that Can Grande was one of the few leaders capable of driving the avaricious popes out of the affairs of the empire and back into their proper sphere of religious rule. It has also been considered that the greyhound symbolizes the eventual reign of the church on earth, conquering the vices symbolized by the beasts on the mountain.

The entire canto is characterized by a note of fear: Dante's natural fear of the dark wood, his superstitious fear of the three beasts, and the apprehension caused by Virgil's description of the journey through Hell. This is counterbalanced in some measure by Dante's view of the sunlight on the mountain, his equally superstitious hope that he will be saved from the beasts because the sun is in the sign of Aries, believed to be its location at the time of Creation, and by the promise of Virgil that he will see Heaven.

The *Comedy* is a long poem of 100 cantos, and each of the three divisions has 33 cantos. Therefore we must view the first canto as the introduction to the entire *Comedy,* not just to the *Inferno.* It sets the scene and starts the poets on their long, long journey.

Summary

It is near the end of the day. Dante gives a short invocation to the Muses, then asks Virgil if he considers him worthy of making the long and arduous journey. Dante recalls others who, while living, have been permitted to visit the realms of the dead — Aeneas, St. Paul — and compares himself unfavorably with them.

Virgil replies by telling him of the great concern for him of a certain angelic spirit, namely Beatrice; and Virgil relates the conversation between them when she descended to Limbo. Beatrice, he says, had been sent by the Virgin Mary, through her messenger St. Lucia, to ask Virgil's help in bringing Dante back from his wanderings. Beatrice wept as she spoke, and Virgil eagerly rescued Dante and began the journey with him for her sake.

Virgil tells Dante to have courage, because the three ladies of Heaven care for him. Dante immediately puts his fears behind him and tells Virgil that he has inspired him to continue on the way. Virgil moves off, and Dante follows.

Commentary

If the first canto acts as an introduction to the entire poem, then Canto 2 is the introduction to the *Inferno* proper. It begins with an invocation; in all of the classic epics — the *Iliad,* the *Odyssey,* and the *Aeneid* — the poem begins with an invocation to the Muses or to some other type of deity. Thus Dante in the *Inferno* uses an invocation to the Muses, to Genius, and to Memory. One might ask why, in a poem that is obviously Christian, Dante does not invoke the aid of Christian deities. The answer should be obvious: he *does* invoke Christian deities in *Purgatorio* and *Paradiso.* But in an invocation concerning Hell, one does not invoke Christian aid.

Dante's traditional invocation to the Muses is very brief indeed; his references to Memory almost seem a longer invocation. The background of the action is given, and Dante portrays himself as a frightened and humble man. The two others he mentions as going before him through Hell are symbolic of his two great concerns: the church and the empire.

The Chosen Vessel is St. Paul, and the reference is to his vision of Hell, as recorded in a widely circulated work of the Middle Ages. The father of Sylvius was Aeneas, who descended into Hell to consult his father Anchises and learn of the future greatness of his people, the Romans. This preoccupation with the church and the empire will continue through the entire *cantica.*

Virgil's account of Beatrice is an interesting one. This is the only canto in the *Inferno* where she is mentioned by name; nor is Jesus *ever* mentioned by name in this unholy place—only by allusion. This indeed is one of the punishments of Hell: that the condemned know God, but have forfeited the right to call upon Jesus as their redeemer.

CANTO 3

Summary

The inscription over the Gate of Hell moves Dante to comment on it. Virgil answers, reminding Dante to have courage and telling him that this is the place he had spoken of earlier. He takes Dante's hand and leads him in to a dark and starless place of such terrible noise that it makes Dante weep.

The unending cries make Dante ask where they come from, and Virgil replies that these are the souls of the uncommitted, who lived for themselves alone, and of the angels who were not rebellious against God, but neither were they faithful to Satan. Neither Heaven nor Hell would have them, and so they must remain here with the selfish, forever running behind a banner, eternally stung by hornets and wasps. Worms at their feet are fed by the blood and tears of these beings.

Dante sees the shore of a river ahead, with people standing and eagerly awaiting passage, and he questions Virgil. Virgil replies that Dante will know the answers when they reach the shore, and Dante remains silent, believing he has offended Virgil with his questions.

As they reach the stream Acheron, they see the boatman, who shouts at the spirits. He tells them that he is to take them to a place from which they can never escape, but he orders Dante to leave because Dante is still living. Virgil answers Charon, saying it had been willed in Heaven that Dante should make this journey.

Charon remains silent, but the cursing, weeping spirits are ordered aboard by the boatman, who strikes with his oars any soul who hesitates. The boat crosses, but before it has landed, the opposite shore is again crowded with condemned souls. Virgil gently explains to Dante (calling him "my son") that the condemned souls come here from every country and that they are impelled by Divine Justice to cross the river into Hell, where, as in life, their fear of retribution is stilled by their desire for their particular sin. He says, also, that Dante can be comforted by Charon's first refusal to carry him on the boat, for only condemned spirits come this way.

As Virgil finishes his explanation, a sudden earthquake, accompanied by wind and flashing fire from the ground, so terrifies Dante that he faints.

Commentary

The inscription over the gate of Hell has a powerful impact: "Abandon hope, all ye who enter here." Dante naturally thinks this applies also to him, and, in the first of many passages which bring a breath of life to the figures of the poets, Virgil smiles and reassures him.

The inscription implies the horror of total despair. It suggests that anyone may enter into Hell at any time — and then all hope is lost. Dante cries out that this sentence is difficult for him to bear. He is using the word in two senses: first, the sentence (with subject and verb) whose meaning is unnerving to him and, second, the sentence as of a judge who has condemned him to abandon all hope. This condemnation does not apply to Dante because allegorically it is still possible for him to achieve salvation, and realistically he is not yet dead so it will not (necessarily) apply to him at all.

Beginning with this canto Dante is setting up the intellectual structure of Hell. Hell is the place for those who deliberately, intellectually, and consciously chose an evil way of life, whereas Paradise is a place of reward for those who consciously chose a righteous way of life. If Hell, then, is a place for the man who made a deliberate and intentional choice of the wrong way, there must be a place for those people who refused to choose either evil or good. Therefore the vestibule of Hell is for those people who refused to make a choice. They are the uncommitted of the world, and having been indecisive in life, that is, never coming to make a choice for themselves, they are constantly stung into movement.

This is the first example of the law of retribution as applied by Dante, where the uncommitted race endlessly after a wavering (and blank) banner. Because they were unwilling to shed their blood for any worthy cause in life, now it is shed unwillingly, to fall to the ground as food for worms. Dante is terrified by the overpowering noise of this dark and starless place. Again and again he will mention noise, as though it were a part, rather than a result, of the punishment of Hell.

Among the sinners are the fallen angels who supported neither God nor Lucifer, but refused to commit themselves and stayed neutral. A refusal to choose is in itself a choice, an idea used by Dante which has since become central in the existentialist philosophy of Jean Paul Sartre.

Dante spies Pope Celestine V, who "made the great refusal" of giving up the chair of Peter after only five months, thereby clearing the way for Boniface VIII, to whom Dante was an implacable enemy. Celestine preferred to return to the obscurity of noncommitment rather than face the problems of the papacy.

The abrupt opening of the canto, with the poets just outside the gate of Hell, brings up the question of how they got there, but there is no answer. After revealing an almost feminine weakness here, Dante gains courage later, in the face of unknown horrors, until he can face even Satan with something like equanimity.

In this early canto, Dante has given examples of two other themes which will continue through the story: the mythological character and the formal incantation of Virgil, the white magician. Charon is a familiar figure in this aspect of ferryman, although in mythology his domain is sometimes the Styx, which in the *Inferno* does not appear until Canto 7, and with a different boatman. When Charon refuses to take Dante across the river it is because his job is to take only the dead who have no chance of salvation. Dante, however, is both a living man and one who still has the possibility of achieving salvation. In some of the later cantos the mythological figures, and even the figure of Satan, are much changed from the usual concept of them.

Virgil's incantation, "Thus it is willed there, where what is willed can be done," is a circumlocution to avoid the word "Heaven," and is repeated in Canto 5. In later cantos other periphrases of various kinds are used.

The shore of the river Acheron (river of Sorrows) is crowded with more souls than Dante believed possible, souls propelled not alone by the anger of Charon but by the sharp prod of divine justice, until they desire to make the crossing; actually this is their final choice, for their desire for sin on earth was also of their own choosing.

In lines 121-25, Dante again emphasizes that Hell is for those who chose it. Only once in the poem (Canto 33) does Dante ever suggest that the choice is irrevocable, and that if you commit an act of sin you will be automatically condemned to Hell. The entire theological basis of Hell is that it is for those who died unrepentant of their sins. As the poet says, it is for those who have died in the wrath of God. Dante leaves room for men to repent of their sins, enter into Purgatory, and later achieve salvation. Hell is filled with people who at the moment of death were either unrepentant or were still committing the same sins. This suggests that the sinners in Hell seem to long for the punishment that is reserved for them.

When Dante looks upon the number of people he sees in the vestibule, he makes the statement that he had not known that Death had undone so many people. In other words, Dante sees many irresolute, indecisive, uncommitted people in the vestibule, and had not realized that so many people had even lived, much less died, without choosing the path of righteousness, or any path at all. The line is interesting because in T. S. Eliot's modern poem *The Wasteland*, Eliot has a character walking through one of the streets in the Wasteland, repeating the same thought.

CANTO 4

Summary

Dante is awakened by loud thunder. He has been in a deep sleep for some time: his eyes are rested, and he finds himself in a strange place, on the brink of an abyss so deep he cannot see the bottom. Virgil says it is time to descend, but Dante notices his pallor and believes that Virgil is afraid. If he, who has been a source of strength to Dante, fears the descent, how can he expect Dante to follow?

Virgil explains that he is pale, not from fear, but from pity for those who are below them. He urges Dante to hurry, for the way is long. They move to the first circle.

Dante hears no sound but the quiet sighs of sadness from those confined in this circle. His guide explains that these are the souls of those who had led blameless lives, but were not baptized. Virgil himself is one of this group, those who lived before Christianity, and whose sadness comes only from being unable to see God. Dante expresses his sorrow, for he knows good men who are confined in Limbo. He asks Virgil if any soul had ever gone out from this place to the realm of the blessed, and Virgil enumerates those liberated by Jesus when he descended into Hell.

The two poets have been walking during this conversation, and pass by the wood of Limbo. Dante sees a fire ahead and realizes that figures of honor rest near it. He asks Virgil why these are honored by separation from the other spirits, and Virgil replies that their fame on earth has gained them this place.

A voice hails Virgil's return, and the two poets are approached by the shades of Homer, Horace, Ovid, and Lucan. Virgil tells Dante their names, then turns away to talk with them. After a time, the group salutes Dante, saying they regard him as one of their number. The entire group moves ahead, talking of subjects which Dante will not disclose, and they come to a castle with seven walls surrounded by a small stream.

They pass over the stream and through the seven gates and reach a green meadow. Dante recognizes the figures of authority dwelling there, and as the poets stand on a small hill, he gives the names of rulers, philosophers, and others who are there, and regrets that he does not have time to name them all. Prominent among the philosophers are Socrates, Plato, Cicero, Seneca, and "the master of those who know" (Aristotle). Now Dante and Virgil leave this quiet place and come to one where there is no light.

Commentary

Dante again underlines the human Virgil, who turns pale with pity. Virgil has made this journey once before, so he knows the torments which are taking place below. More important, he is approaching the place where he himself dwells and will remain through all eternity, and Dante echoes the sadness of the place — which Virgil knows only too well — when he says he knows many good men who dwell here in Limbo.

When Dante states that he is awakened from his swoon by a heavy peal of thunder, we should be aware that it is not really thunder but instead is the horrible cry emerging from the great pit of Hell—the cry of all the damned souls heard as one. This is the only time that Dante is able to see Hell in its entirety. In the future cantos, and later in this canto, he will hear only the cries and sounds of the sinners who are confined to each individual circle of Hell, but here he is awakened by the hopeless sounds of all Hell emerging, and sounding like terrible peals of thunder. In contrast to this, when Dante reaches this first circle of Hell there is silence—total silence. No sound comes from this circle. This is because those who are confined to Limbo are not being punished, and the silence is a silence of dignity.

Between Hell proper, that is, the place of punishment, and the vestibule, Dante places the circle of Limbo, devoted to those people who had no opportunity to choose either good or evil in terms of having faith in Christ. This circle is occupied by the virtuous pagans, those who lived before Christ was born, and by the unbaptized.

The virtuous pagans had lived blameless lives, and they are judged and honored according to their virtue. They exist here according to what they had themselves envisioned as a life after death. This may be illustrated by turning to one of the dialogues of Socrates. At the end of the *Apology,* Socrates speaks of the afterlife in which he envisions the migration of the soul to a place where that soul can spend an eternity talking with great people who have gone before him or who live at the present moment.

Thus we see Socrates in Limbo discussing philosophy and ethics with the great souls who are there. In other words, Socrates has attained the kind of afterlife which he, as a wise man, envisioned as the perfect one. It is not a punishment; it is the failure of the imagination to envision the coming of the Christ and the faith that man should have in the coming of a Messiah. Thus when Virgil was just dead, he records that someone "in power crowned" appeared in Hell and took from there the shades of all the ancient patriarchs of the Old Testament, who had faith that the Messiah would some day come.

On the allegorical level, the fact that these pagans in Limbo lived a highly virtuous, or ethical, or moral life, and are still in Limbo, implies that no amount of humanistic endeavor, no amount of virtue or knowledge, ethics or morality, can save or redeem one who has not had faith in Christ, and, having faith in Christ, has been openly baptized and is in a state of grace. For Dante, good works, virtue, or morality count for nothing if one has not acknowledged Christ as the redeemer.

Note, finally, that Hell is a place where the person is given no further opportunity to choose. He has made the choice long before.

CANTO 5

Summary

Dante has moved down to the second circle, smaller than the first, which forms the real beginning of Hell. The grinning Minos sits at the entrance judging condemned souls, and the circles of his tail around his body indicate the place in Hell where a spirit is to go for punishment. There is a constant crowd of spirits around him, coming to him for judgment and being carried down the circles of Hell.

Minos cautions Dante against entering, but Virgil silences him, first by asking him why he too questions Dante (as Charon did), then by telling him, in the same words he used to Charon, that it had been willed in Heaven that Dante should make this journey. (The word "Heaven" is not used, here or anywhere else in Hell.)

Dante beholds a place completely dark, in which there is noise worse than that of a storm at sea. Lamenting, moaning, shrieking, the spirits are whirled and swept by an unceasing storm; Dante learns that these are the spirits doomed by carnal lust. He asks the names of some who are blown past, and Virgil answers with their names and something of their stories.

Then Dante asks particularly to speak to two who are together, and Virgil tells him to call them to him in the name of love. They come, and one thanks Dante for his pity and wishes him peace, then tells their story. She reveals first that a lower circle of Hell waits for the man who murdered them. With bowed head, Dante tells Virgil he is thinking of the "sweet thoughts and desires" that had brought the lovers to this place. Calling Francesca by name, he asks her to explain how she and her lover were lured into sin.

Francesca replies that it was a book of the romance of Lancelot that caused their downfall. They were alone, reading it aloud, and so many parts of the book seemed to tell of their own love. They kissed, and the book was forgotten. During her story, the other spirit has been weeping bitterly, and Dante is so moved by pity, he also weeps—and faints.

Commentary

This second circle is the true beginning of Hell. Here Minos sits as judge, but unlike Charon, this grotesque creature is not the Minos of mythology, the great king (or line of kings) who ruled the fabled isle of Crete. The formal incantation of Canto 3 is repeated here and silences the protests of Minos.

This is the circle of carnal lust, first of the four circles of incontinence. The sinners are tossed and whirled by the winds, as in life they felt themselves helpless in the tempests of passion. This canto begins the circles devoted to the sins of incontinence: the sins of the appetite, the sins of self-indulgence, the sins of passion. These are also the sins of the person who has a weakness of will: here are those who did not make a "resolute choice" for good; those who yielded too easily to temptation; and those who did not remain steadfast in searching out goodness.

Before Dante sees the sinners, he first comes upon the judge of all Hell, Minos, before whom all of the condemned spirits come. When a new spirit arrives in Hell, it immediately confesses all of its past sins and by this confession gains a self-knowledge of the sin. In Hell there can be no more self-deception. But the irony is that these souls, being damned, can no longer benefit from the knowledge of their sins. Thus their confession is also a kind of damnation for them.

Minos, like the other guardians of Hell, does not want to admit Dante, a living being still capable of redemption. But he is forced to do so by Virgil. Among those whom Dante sees in this circle are people like Cleopatra, Dido, and Helen. Some of these women, besides being adulteresses, have also committed suicide. The question immediately arises as to why they are not deeper down in Hell in the circle reserved for suicides. We must remember that in Dante's Hell a person is judged by his own standards, that is, by the standards of the society in which he lived. For example, in classical times suicide was not considered a sin, but adultery was. Therefore the spirit is judged by the ethics by which he lived and is condemned for adultery, not suicide.

One of the loveliest of images is given in Dante's simile of the cranes, and Francesca's gentle words, beginning with line 100, are touching with their repetition of "love . . . love . . . love. . . ." However, Dante still retains some of the artificial, posturing attitude of the poet of courtly love. As his technique grows more sure in later cantos, it will be seen that the language and style of the spirits' stories becomes more definitely their own and not Dante's. In telling the tale of Paolo and Francesca, Dante is following the tradition of the poets of courtly love, and the language reveals it. He has, however, given the story the human, individual touch of his "sweet new style," which has made it one of the best-known episodes of the *Comedy*.

Dante sees Paolo and Francesca, and calls them to him in the name of love—a mild conjuration at Virgil's insistence. Francesca tells their story; Paolo can only weep. Francesca da Rimini was the wife of Gianciotto, the deformed older brother of Paolo, who was a beautiful youth. The marriage had been one of alliance and had continued for some ten years when Paolo and Francesca were surprised in the compromising situation described in the poem. Gianciotto promptly murdered them both, for which he will be confined in the lowest circle of Hell.

For modern readers, it is sometimes difficult to understand why Dante considered adultery, or lustfulness, the least hateful of the sins of incontinence. It is important to understand Dante's reasoning: as the intellectual basis of Hell, Dante conceived of Hell as a place where the sinner deliberately chose his sin and failed to repent of it. This is particularly true of the lower circles of malice and fraud. Here, however, Francesca did not *deliberately* choose adultery; hers was a gentle lapsing into love for Paolo; a matter of incontinence, of weakness of will. Only the fact that she was killed by her husband in the moment of adultery allowed her no opportunity to repent, and for this reason she is condemned to Hell.

By this means, Dante seeks to show the difference in the enormity of the sins and therefore the placing of these adulterers in this higher circle. The sin of adultery committed over and over in deliberate assignations would be placed in the lower part of Hell, in the circle reserved for sexual perverts. It would then properly be called concupiscence. But Francesca's sin is not of this type. She is passionate, certainly she is capable of sin and she is certainly guilty of sin, but she represents the woman whose only concern is the man she loves, not her immortal soul. She found her only happiness in his love, and of course, now her misery. Her love had been her heaven; it is now her hell.

Francesca feels that love is something that does not need to be justified. It is a case, not of depravity or concupiscence, not of some vulgar sexual sin, but of a woman who has drifted helplessly — though willingly — into love. Someone like Francesca, who even in Hell retains those essential characteristics of the feminine being — her modesty, her delicate expression of feeling — arouses in us nothing but sympathy for her plight. She is kind, she is graceful, she is gentle, and in spite of her being in Hell, there is still a sense of modesty and of charm. It is these qualities which cause Dante to faint at the end of the canto after hearing her story.

In this love of Paolo and Francesca there is desire, delicate fancy, tenderness, and human frailty — and there is the mark of tragedy. And Dante, who has entered the realm of eternity carrying with him the whole of his humanity, as a Christian must indeed condemn the sinners, but as a man is captivated and saddened, and his eyes fill with tears when Francesca says quietly, "We read no more." One cannot help being moved by the lovers, particularly Francesca, who cannot bless Dante, but can only wish him peace — a peace she and her lover will never know in this tempestuous place, though they are together forever. No bitterness is greater than this, to remember happiness when one is in a state of wretchedness, so that remembering causes bitter torment.

In Hell the sinners retain all of those qualities for which they were damned, and they remain the same throughout eternity, that is, the soul is depicted in Hell with those exact characteristics which condemned him to Hell in the first place. Consequently, as Francesca loved Paolo in this world, throughout eternity she will love him in Hell. But they are damned, they will not change, they will never cease to love, and they can never be redeemed. And this is represented metaphorically by placing Paolo close to Francesca and by having the two of them being buffeted about together through this circle of Hell for eternity.

By reading the story of Francesca, we can perhaps understand better the intellectual basis by which Dante depicts the other sins in Hell. He chooses a character who represents a sin; then he expresses poetically the person who committed the sin. Francesca is not perhaps truly representative of the sin of this circle, and "carnal lust" seems a harsh term for her feelings, but Dante has chosen her story to make his point: that the sin here is a sin of incontinence, of weakness of the will, of falling from grace through inaction of conscience. Many times in Hell Dante will respond sympathetically, or with pity, to some of these lost souls.

CANTO 6

Summary

Dante regains consciousness, to find himself in the third circle, witnessing a new torment: endless cold rain mixed with hail and snow, falling on the ground which gives off a terrible stench.

Cerberus, the three-headed monster, stands over those sunk deep in the slush. He barks furiously, and claws and bites all within reach. These spirits howl in the rain and attempt to evade the monster. Seeing the two travelers, Cerberus turns on them and is silenced only when Virgil throws handfuls of the reeking dirt into his three mouths.

Dante and Virgil pass by him, walking on the shades who lie on the ground and who seem to Dante to have physical bodies. Only one spirit is not on the ground, and it speaks to Dante as one who knew him in life. Dante, however, cannot recognize him and asks him to tell his name and why he is here. The shade says he was a citizen of Florence, a city full of envy, and was known to Dante as Ciacco (the Hog). For his well-known gluttony, he was doomed to his third circle of Hell.

Dante expresses his sympathy, and then asks the fate of Florence and why it is so divided now. Ciacco foretells a future war and the defeat and expulsion of one party. He concludes his prophecy, and Dante asks where certain good citizens of Florence can now be found. Ciacco tells him that they are much further down in Hell, for worse crimes than his, and that Dante will see them if he travels that far. He also asks Dante to speak of him when he returns to earth, then, refusing to say more, he looks sideways at Dante and falls to the ground.

Virgil tells Dante that Ciacco will now remain as he is until the Last Judgment, and they talk of the future life. Dante questions Virgil concerning the Last Judgment, and Virgil answers that, although these souls will never reach perfection, they will be nearer to it after the Last Judgment than before and therefore will feel more pain as well as more pleasure.

Commentary

Dante awakens in the third circle, that of the gluttons. Again, he has been borne unconscious to this place, still in the region of the incontinent.

Cerberus guards the place, and as in mythology, he requires a sop for each of his three mouths (this time the foul mud of the circle will suffice) before he will permit passage. With this constant hunger, he is a fitting guardian for the circle of gluttons, who transformed their lives into a continual feast and did nothing but eat and drink and now lie like pigs in the mire.

In the intellectual progression down through Hell we move from the circle of lust, a type of sin that was mutual or shared, to the third circle, that of sin performed in isolation. The glutton is one of uncontrolled appetite, one who deliberately, in his own solitary way, converted natural foods into a sort of god, or at least an object of worship. So now his punishment is a reversal, and instead of eating the fine delicate foods and wines of the world, he is forced to eat filth and mud. Instead of sitting in his comfortable house relishing all of the sensual aspects of good food and good wine and good surroundings, he lies in the foul rain.

Aside from brief mention in earlier cantos, this is Dante's first political allusion, and it takes the form of an outburst from Ciacco. The voice is Ciacco's, but the words are Dante's. Ciacco's prophecies are the first of many political predictions which recur in the *Divine Comedy* and especially in the *Inferno*. Since the imaginary journey takes place in 1300, Dante relates, as prophecies, events which had already occurred at the time the poem was being composed.

Curiously, Ciacco falls into what might be called unconsciousness, from which he will not awaken, Virgil says, until Judgment Day. One wonders why this privilege of release from torment is given him; surely not for his political harangue, which is surpassed in bitterness by other spirits in the cantica. Perhaps Dante's acquaintance with Ciacco in life, as a jolly companion, would be enough to permit poetic license, but not to permit his exclusion from Hell.

Another note may be useful. The souls in this upper part of Hell often wish to be remembered to people in the world. But as we descend deeper into Hell the souls wish to conceal the fact that they are in Hell and have no desire to be remembered on earth. For example, the glutton is often depicted as a happy-go-lucky, charming person whom it is a pleasure to be around. Thus Ciacco wishes Dante to speak of him to his friends when he returns to earth. But the sins of those lower in Hell are more vicious, and these souls do *not* wish to be remembered in the world.

The conversation between Dante and Virgil concerning the day of judgment is based upon the philosophy of Aristotle as expounded by St.

32

Thomas Aquinas, who wrote that "The soul without the body hath not the perfection of its nature." Virgil explains that after the day of judgment the shades will be *nearer* perfection because their souls will be reunited with their bodies. They will not, however, *achieve* perfection – that is, salvation – and will, according to the doctrine of Aquinas, feel more pain after Judgment Day, as well as more pleasure: "The more a thing is perfect, the more it feels pleasure and likewise pain."

CANTO 7

Summary

Plutus challenges the travelers with unintelligible words, but Virgil tells Dante to keep up his courage; nothing can stop them from descending. Plutus has swelled to terrifying size. However, when Virgil tells him their journey is willed in Heaven, he falls limply to the ground, and the poets descend to the fourth circle, where Dante witnesses new torments.

Comparing the actions of these souls to the whirlpool Charybdis, Dante watches as the two groups roll great weights halfway around the circle, where they crash into one another and, each blaming the other, turn back only to clash again on the other side of the circle, one group crying, "Why grasp?" and the other, "Why squander?"

Dante asks the identity of the many tonsured spirits, and Virgil replies that they were priests and popes and cardinals, who sinned greatly either in avarice or prodigality, the opposite vices in the management of worldly goods.

Dante is surprised that he cannot recognize any of the figures, but Virgil explains that as in life they showed no discernment, so now the distinction of their features is dimmed beyond recognition. He adds a warning against greed for gold, the goods of Fortune, since no amount of gold can now stop the punishment of these spirits.

Dante asks what Fortune is, that she should hold all the good things of the world, and Virgil, disgusted at the foolishness of greedy men, delivers his judgment of her: Fortune (Luck) was ordained by Heaven as guardian or overseer of the wealth of the world. Some persons and nations have a greater share of this wealth, others a lesser one, but the balance is changing constantly. Fortune is the maker of her own laws in her own realm, as the other gods are in theirs; she cannot be understood and does not hear those who curse her, but goes her own way.

Virgil then reminds Dante that time has passed quickly, and they must descend to another circle. They cross to the other bank and find a fountain of strange, dark water which flows in a stream down through a crack in the rock. Following this to the foot of the rocks, they come to the marsh called Styx.

Here Dante finds people immersed in mud, striking at one another with hands, feet, and head, and biting one another. Virgil tells him that he is looking at souls destroyed by anger and that more lie under the waters of Styx, making bubbles with each cry. Virgil repeats their words, which cannot be fully understood. They are telling of the sullenness of their lives, when they should have been happy in the light of the sun, and now they live sullen forever.

The two poets circle the edge of the marsh and finally reach the base of a tower.

Commentary

Plutus, legendary god of riches, appropriately guards the fourth circle, the abode of the prodigal (the spendthrifts) and of the avaricious (the misers). Although his words are commonly held to be gibberish, a little stretch of the imagination can translate them into a cry for Satan's assistance. Plutus swells with rage (perhaps symbolic of the overinflated importance given to riches?) but promptly collapses when Virgil repeats a variation of the incantation he used in Canto 3 and again in Canto 5.

Dante compares the action of the sinners in the circle to the dreaded whirlpool Charybdis and its surrounding waters. The useless efforts with which the sinners push the huge stones represent the futile persistence they practiced in gathering worldly goods during their lives.

The question immediately arises as to why Dante places hoarders and spendthrifts in a circle lower than the gluttons. That is, why is hoarding and spending more horrible than mere gluttony? The gluttons misused the natural products of the world, which, for Dante, was not so bad as the misers and spendthrifts, who hoarded and had no respect for the man-made objects of this world, that is, money and property. The distinction, however, is not vitally important. What is poetically significant is that these two types of people were opposites in life, thus the punishment for them in Hell is the mutual antagonism that they have after death. A miser could not understand someone who spent money wildly, so in Hell these people are pitted against each other.

The Styx is called a marsh; in mythology it was a river (the river of Hate), one of the five rivers of Hades, and its boatman was Charon. The source of the Styx is described rather fully by Dante. The Styx serves a double purpose. It separates the upper Hell from the nether Hell, and it also functions as the circle for the wrathful. As the wrathful people were hateful during their lifetime, they are now in a river of hate. These people are divided into two categories. First is the open and violent hatred, and the punishment is that they strike out at each other in almost any fashion; the second type of hatred is the slow, sullen hatred. The punishment for this type is that they are choking on their own rage, gurgling in the filth of Styx, unable to express themselves as they become choked on their own malevolent hatred. Virgil's words quoting the lament of the sullen comprise one of the brief passages that come through beautifully in translation.

Thus with the end of the sins of the incontinent we have completed a pattern, beginning where adultery is a weakness of the will and therefore not intended to hurt another, through the circle of gluttony, miserliness, and waste—types of sins committed in isolation—and finally approaching the worst of the sins of the incontinent, the wrathful, who by their hatred *can* possibly harm someone.

CANTOS 8-9

Summary

As Dante and Virgil were approaching the tower, they saw two fires, which were answered by a signal flame in the far distance. Dante now asks the reason for the beacons and who made them. Virgil tells him to look into the mist and he will see the answer. Dante sees a little boat coming swiftly toward them, with only one oarsman, who challenges them. Virgil replies that he, Phlegyas, complains for nothing, since he must only carry them across the water.

Although Phlegyas is in a towering rage, Virgil enters the boat. Dante follows, noting that he alone has any weight and that this causes the prow of the boat to dip as they cross the water.

Before they reach the shore, a muddy figure rises up and tries to attack Dante, asking why he is here when he is not yet dead. There is an exchange of words between the spirit and Dante, who at first does not know him. The shade informs Dante that he weeps endlessly here in the mud, and Dante, in sudden recognition, wishes that he may remain so and curses him.

Virgil praises Dante for his action, and tells him that others now alive think themselves great will come to the same end as this spirit. Dante expresses a wish to see the spirit sink into the Stygian marsh, and is told that this will happen before they reach the shore. He looks back, and to his satisfaction Filippo Argenti is attacked by others in the circle of the wrathful.

Virgil tells Dante that ahead is the city of Dis, with many inhabitants, and when Dante remarks on the red glow of its structures, Virgil tells him this is the eternal fire of Hell.

The boat circles the walls, which seem to be made of iron, and the boatman orders them out at the entrance. Above the gates, Dante sees the rebellious angels, who angrily ask why he is in the realm of the dead. Virgil quiets them by indicating he wishes to talk with them. They reply that they will speak only with him and that Dante must return the way he came, if he can find the way alone.

Dante realizes he can never return without a guide and begs Virgil, who has saved him so often, to end their journey here if they are not allowed to go on together and to return with him by the same path.

Virgil reassures him, again, that no one can stop their journey and asks him to remain where he is, for Virgil will surely not abandon him. Dante is left behind in a very doubtful state of mind, for he cannot hear the conversation. It is a short one, however, for the angels rush back and slam the gates shut. Virgil returns to Dante, sighing because the fallen angels bar the way. However, he tells Dante of the approach of one who will open the gates.

Virgil listens intently, because he cannot see through the heavy mist. He regrets they could not enter the gates by themselves, but help has been promised, though it seems long delayed. Dante is much alarmed and asks his guide, in a roundabout way, if anyone from the upper circles has ever made this descent. Virgil answers that he himself had once been sent to summon a shade from the circle of Judas, far below here, so he knows the way well.

Dante's attention turns to the tower, where three bloody Furies now stand. Their heads are covered with snakes instead of hair, and Virgil gives their names. Dante cowers near his master as the Furies call for Medusa, so that the sight of her will turn Dante to stone.

Because Dante is still mortal, and Medusa *can* petrify him (literally), Virgil turns him around with his back to the wall and tells him to cover his eyes and then puts his own hands over Dante's. Dante comments briefly upon the hidden meaning of what has happened, and of what is to come.

A noise like a hurricane causes the poets to look toward Styx, and they see a figure crossing without touching the marsh. Spirits rush away from him, and he moves his left hand before him to dispel the fog of the marsh.

Dante recognizes the heavenly messenger, and Virgil asks him to remain quiet and bow down. The angry messenger reaches the gate, which opens at the touch of his wand. He then reproves the insolent angels for trying to stop what is willed in Heaven and reminds them of the injuries suffered by Cerberus when he was dragged to the upper world.

The messenger turns, and without speaking, goes back across the marsh, intent upon other cares. The two poets enter the city, and Dante sees a wide plain covered with sepulchers. They are red hot, and flames come from their open tops. Dante hears terrible cries and asks their source, and Virgil replies that these are the tombs of the numerous arch-heretics. They turn to the right, and walk between the wall and the tombs.

Commentary

The first stanza of Canto 8 is probably the source for the tradition that Dante wrote the first seven cantos of the *Comedy* before his exile.

This appears to be almost the only evidence. There is, however, little unity in the canto. It is weak in construction; too much happens: there is a signal given, a boat appears, Virgil has a short argument with the boatman, and Dante a fierce one with Filippo Argenti, and so on. Why Argenti should be singled out for mention remains an enigma, but he was apparently a bitter enemy of Dante's and reveals himself as a man marked by all the passions, hatreds, and loves of his time.

The marsh of Styx is the fifth circle. When Dante enters the boat to cross it, he mentions for the first time the fact of his physical weight. Later this causes the spirits of other circles to realize that Dante is still alive.

The marsh is crossed with unseemly haste, and the city of Dis looms ahead. As they approach the city, they are leaving the first division of Hell, that of incontinence, and entering the realm of malice, the sins of the will. Dante uses the word "mosques" to describe the towers of the city because the teachings of Mohammed were considered a Christian heresy rather than a separate religion. The fallen angels who oppose the poets' entrance to the city are said by Virgil to be the same ones who tried to prevent Jesus from entering the gate of Hell.

As Dante descends in the circles of Hell, he will gradually lose his sympathy and his pity, and as one of the spirits of the damned provokes him he will retaliate with a certain degree of violence. The first indication of this is in Canto 8 when Dante turns on Filippo Argenti in such a furious manner. This does not mean that Dante cannot respond with sympathy to some of the spirits, but in Hell the sin of the person evokes from Dante a certain righteous indignation, and he responds sometimes with violence.

In Canto 9, Dante returns to his customary style and grasp of his material. There is a short passage of dramatic impact: Virgil, the fearless guide, stands pale and helpless, speaking brokenly to himself. His incantations, and his reason, are useless against those who willfully dared to oppose Jesus himself, and Virgil is forced to ask for the help which has been promised. Allegorically, this is another reminder that human reason cannot achieve salvation without divine aid. Virgil, as reason, cannot understand sin committed in full knowledge and with deliberate will.

Dante, in a touching manner, asks a diplomatic question designed to change his master's train of thought—and perhaps quiet his own fears. Virgil relates the story of his earlier journey down to the circle of Judecca. This took place not long after Virgil's death, he says, when Erichtho, the sorceress, at the insistence of Sextius Pompeius, summoned Virgil to bring a spirit from the circle of Judecca to foretell the outcome of a battle.

The story of Erichtho's sorcery was related by Lucan and concerns the battle of Pharsalia, between Julius Caesar and Pompey the Great, which was fought in 48 B.C. Lucan of course did not mention Virgil's name in this connection, and no doubt medieval legend added the name of Virgil because he had told the story of the descent of Aeneas into Hell. A curious discrepancy arises from Dante's use of the tale, however, because Virgil was still alive at the time of the battle of Pharsalia.

Dante's attention has been diverted to the activity on the city walls. The figures of the Furies are the same as found in the myths, and the threat of showing Medusa to Dante is a strong reminder that Dante is still alive. There is an obscure reference to the lesson to be learned from this episode. Its general meaning is that a guilty conscience (the Furies) and a hard heart (Medusa) stand in the way of salvation; that reason (Virgil) may be of help but only if joined by divine aid (the Heavenly Messenger). The complex and dramatic action of Canto 9 is expressed with a more mature art which transforms the symbols into concrete and realistic images. We experience with Dante his tension and his expectation of divine help, his confidence and his anxiety, and finally his relief at the arrival of the messenger from Heaven.

The figure of the angelic messenger is not described as we should expect, a resplendent, winged creature. His physical attributes are purposely left undefined. The impression of his approach is conveyed through two dramatic figures of speech. His bursting open the barred gates with a light touch is impressive. His haughty speech to the fiends and his abrupt departure are expressive of his hatred for the abhorrent place.

CANTO 10

Summary

As the poets travel the secret path, Dante asks if he may speak with one of the spirits, since all the tombs are open. Virgil replies that they will be closed forever after the Last Judgment, but that Dante's wish will be granted and so will the wish he has not expressed. Dante answers that he did not want to conceal anything but only wanted to stop asking so many questions, since his master had indicated that this questioning troubled him.

Dante is startled by a voice, identified by Virgil as that of Farinata, which tells them to turn and they will see him. Dante looks, and Virgil urges him forward to the edge of Farinata's tomb and tells him to be brief in his conversation.

The haughty Farinata is sitting upright and inquires about Dante's ancestors. The poet answers. The shade then says that he was their enemy and twice defeated them, but Dante replies that they returned both times, which was more than Farinata's party had been able to do.

The argument is interrupted by a spirit in another tomb, who recognizes Dante and believes he is making the journey because of the greatness of his poetry. If this is so, he asks, where is his own son and why isn't he on this journey also? Dante replies that he himself is being led by another, whom the poet Guido (the spirit's son) may have disdained. Because Dante has spoken in the past tense, the shade believes his son is dead, and before Dante can answer, it falls back into the tomb.

Farinata's shade resumes the argument exactly where it left off, telling Dante that if his party has not yet returned to power, it is more torture to him than his fiery tomb. He also warns Dante that before the full moon has risen fifty times (that is, within fifty months), his party will return. Then he asks Dante a question: why is the other party so bitterly opposed to his own? And Dante replies that it is because of the fierce battle [at Montaperti] which caused the other party to issue decrees of exile. Farinata says that he was not the only leader in the battles against Florence, but he *was* alone in saving the city from destruction after it was defeated.

Dante, in turn, asks a question. He has noticed that the spirits can look back into the past, or ahead into the future, and tell of what has happened and of what will come to pass; but they do not know what is happening on earth at the present moment, and he wishes to know why this is so. The spirit replies that they are like a person whose sight is defective; they can see only at a distance — God has given them this much light — and they know nothing of the present world.

Dante asks Farinata to tell the spirit of Guido's father that his son still lives; then hearing Virgil call him, he quickly asks the identity of the other spirits who lie nearby. Farinata answers only that Frederick II and "the cardinal" are here and refuses to speak again. Dante is bewildered by this knowledge of the spirits concerning the past and the future. He returns to his guide, and as they move away, Virgil asks why he is so puzzled. Dante tells him, and his master replies that he should remember this, for when they reach the blessed lady she will reveal all of Dante's life, past and future.

They turn to the left, go across the walled city, following a path which goes down into a fetid valley.

Commentary

The city of Dis generally considered as including all of the rest of Hell, from the wall to the pit of Cocytus. It is indeed Satan's own. Here again, there is a difference of opinion among critics, some considering that only this circle of Hell is the city of Dis. Dante's words, beginning with line 70, would seem to confirm this. However, since the heretics are confined here, it seems more probable that Dante's intention was for the city to include all the rest of Hell; otherwise the heretics, whom Dante would consider as devoted to Satan, would be confined in a place much closer to Satan. Dante recognizes many of the figures here but does not disclose the nature of their heresy.

Dante wonders if the tombs are not empty; therefore when Farinata speaks to Dante, Dante cringes partly in fright and and in awe of the great man, and partly because he had not expected a voice to come from these supposedly empty sepulchers. The first words that Farinata speaks inspire a certain amount of sympathy and affection for him. In a fiery bed enclosed in a dreadful tomb, he can still be touched by once again hearing the beloved Tuscan speech, recalling to him cherished memories of his country.

Since Farinata is depicted ultimately as having a very haughty and proud nature, his sentimentality and his love for his country create in our minds a sympathetic feeling for this proud man. At the end of his speech he even suggests that perhaps he, Farinata, caused too much trouble in his own land, that famed country which he says he perhaps "tested too much."

Historically speaking, Farinata was a powerful personality of the preceding generation. He belonged to the opposing political party, the Ghibellines, and Dante's family were Guelphs. As is alluded to in this particular canto, Farinata had twice led the Ghibellines against the Guelphs and had twice defeated them. Thus he and Dante should be bitter enemies. However, this is not someone whom Dante hates; instead Farinata was a person whom Dante admired tremendously: one may respect an enemy even while being opposed to him.

Farinata, along with Cavalcanti, is in the circle of the heretics, partly because both he and Cavalcanti were Epicureans. According to Dante's definition, a heretic was one who chose his own opinion rather than following the judgment of the church; Cavalcanti and Farinata followed the Epicurean philosophy. The Epicureans believed that there is no soul, that everything dies with the body. They regarded the pleasures of this life as the highest goal for man. Since Dante knew both Farinata and Cavalcanti as Epicureans, he had fully expected to meet them in this circle of Hell.

Farinata's concerns are those of a warrior; any other sentiments are meaningless to him. He is a citizen: the request he makes to Dante is uttered in the name of their homeland. He is a partisan: the first question he asks the poet is about his ancestors. He is an invincible warrior: he tells of scattering his opponents twice. Farinata's greatest glory was his love for Florence, a love which withstood every hatred and saved his beloved city. The theme of Cavalcanti's paternal love, interwoven with this heroic one, is very effective from the poetic point of view.

Dante has created an image of Farinata as a very proud person, and also an image of power, character, and strength. He describes Farinata as raising himself erect, so that he could be seen only from the waist up, as though his upper body represents his total personality. This suggests that, spiritually, he towers above all of Hell, and creates an image of infinite strength and grandeur.

The remark about Guido (Cavalcanti) holding Virgil in disdain is a puzzling one. Several explanations have been offered. One of the most logical is that Guido was a supporter of the papacy in its struggle against the empire and would therefore oppose the ideas of Virgil, poet of the empire.

The two figures mentioned are Frederick II, the most versatile and enlightened emperor of the Middle Ages, and Ottaviano degli Ubaldini, a fierce Ghibelline cardinal, who is reported to have said: "If there is any soul, I have lost mine for the Ghibellines."

The movements of the poets at the end of the canto may be somewhat confusing. The city of Dis is completely encircled by its own wall; its center is the circular abyss. Dante and Virgil have been following along the base of the wall, and now they turn left onto a path that strikes across the circle at right angles to the wall and reach the edge of a cliff.

CANTOS 11-12

Summary

The two poets reach a bank made of broken rock, and because of the foul odor, take refuge behind a large stone, the tomb of Pope Anastasius. Virgil remarks that they should stay where they are until they get used to the stench, and Dante asks what they can do to pass the time. His guide had intended to instruct him and tells him what lies below them: first there is a circle of three divisions, or rounds, each filled with condemned souls. Next—because all malice ends in injury and is hated in Heaven—are the fraudulent, confined in a lower circle. This is because only man is capable of fraud, and this is particularly offensive to God.

The first circle below, Virgil continues, is for those who have committed violence against God, against themselves, or against their neighbors. The first round of this seventh circle is for those violent against a neighbor's person or his property, and this includes murderers, assailants, and robbers.

In the second round are those violent against themselves: suicides and those who waste their goods. And in the third and smallest round are those who do violence to God through blasphemy and denial.

In the circle below the violent, the fraudulent are confined, and Virgil gives a long list of those condemned. Finally, in the last and smallest circle, at the bottom of the pit, are held the traitors—for all eternity.

Dante now understands what lies below but asks his master why those guilty of incontinence are punished outside the walls of Dis. Virgil reproves him for not remembering Aristotle's *Ethics,* in which it is explained that incontinence is somewhat less offensive to God (because it is without malice). Dante thanks him for the explanation, then asks another question, concerning usury: why does it so anger God?

Virgil replies that Nature follows the divine plan of God; and art (that is, artisanship, the working of natural resources and the product of labor) follows Nature. Art is, in this sense, the grandchild of God; it was God's intention that man should live by nature and his own art—the labors that he performs—and that the man who seeks to evade this labor goes against the plan of God.

Virgil asks Dante to follow him; it is growing late, and they must walk some distance to the next descent.

The beginning of the descent is rocky and broken, as from an earthquake. The only opening is a cleft in the rock, and it is guarded by the Minotaur. He is in a towering rage, and Virgil taunts him, asking if perhaps he thinks Theseus is here. He orders the monster to remove himself, and while the monster is plunging about in helpless anger, Virgil urges Dante to begin the descent quickly.

It is rocky and steep, and Dante notices that the stones move under his feet because of his weight. He is deep in thought, and Virgil tells him how the walls of the abyss came to be broken and fallen as they are. When he had first been sent (by Erichtho) to the lowest circle of Hell, the walls had been solid and unbroken; just before Jesus descended into Hell, a terrible earthquake shook the valley and the rocks fell, and the walls of the abyss became as they are now.

Virgil tells Dante to look into the valley and he will see the river of boiling blood, in which the violent are confined. Dante sees a wide ditch, and along its bank are centaurs armed with arrows. They see the two poets, and three of them come forward carrying bows and spears. One asks where the poets are from, and why they are here, and threatens them with his bow. Virgil replies that he will speak with Chiron, then tells Dante the names of the three: Nessus, Chrion, and Pholus. They are only three among the thousands who go along the bank and keep the tortured spirits in their proper place in the river of blood.

Dante and Virgil approach the centaurs, and Chiron, moving his beard aside with the end of an arrow, speaks first to his companions. He has seen that the rocks move beneath Dante's feet; therefore Dante is alive. Virgil confirms this and tells the centaur that he is guiding Dante and that they are making the journey because they must, not because they are enjoying it. He explains the visit of the blessed lady and tells Chiron they are not robbers, but require one of the centaurs to guide them to the ford across the river, where Dante must be carried, since he is not a spirit. Chiron sends Nessus to guide them and to guard them from the other centaurs, and the three move along the bank.

Dante sees the shrieking spirits sunk in blood, some even to the eyebrows. Nessus explains that those sunk deepest are the tyrants, and he mentions several. Virgil tells Dante to listen carefully to Nessus, and farther on they see spirits sunk to the neck and one standing alone who, Nessus says, is a murderer. Dante recognizes many standing immersed to the

chest but does not name them. Again the incessant noise is almost in-
tolerable to him.

The river becomes more and more shallow, until some of the spirits
have only their feet covered. The group has reached the ford over the river,
and Nessus stops to tell Dante that on the other side of the ford the river
again becomes deeper and that Attila and others, including highwaymen,
are confined there. Nessus leaves them on the opposite bank of the first
round and returns over the ford.

Commentary

Virgil clearly describes the regions below and then in a long moral
discourse gives the reasons why each sin is punished in progressively lower
circles of Hell.

Note that Dante places the dissipators of their own wealth in the
seventh circle, with the suicides and those who "weep where they should
be joyous." It is sometimes difficult to see the distinction between the dissipators of wealth below and the prodigal of the fourth circle above; between the joyless of the seventh circle and the sullen confined above in the
marsh of Styx. The distinction is in the manner of their sinning: those in the
upper circles sinned in carelessness and without thought; the ones confined
below sinned deliberately and with malice, which emphasizes Dante's concept of Hell, wherein a deliberate intellectual choice is the worst kind of sin.

Dante makes no distinction between violence to the person and violence to property; they are one and the same. The waning of the feudal
system and the rise of commerce had given the citizen of that age, particularly in the great commercial centers, a strong sense of property.

Dante uses the term "usury" in a different sense from the modern one.
It did not mean the charging of exorbitant interest for loaning money; it
meant the charging of *any* interest at all. Strange as it may seem in our own
time, the idea that money makes money was repugnant to Dante, who believed that profits should be fruits of labor. Ironically, his own city of
Florence became one of the principal banking centers of Europe during the
fourteenth century and continued so for several succeeding centuries.

Fraud may be practiced on men who have no cause for placing confidence in those by whom they are defrauded; in this case only the common
bond between man and man is broken. Those who committed this kind of
fraud lie in the eighth circle. But the sinners who perpetrated fraud on those
bound by natural love—such as traitors to kindred, fatherland, guests, and
benefactors—are condemned to the lowest place in Hell, the ninth circle.

With Canto 12, we enter the seventh circle, the circle of violence, with
its three rounds. It begins with the violence of the landslide which broke
and scattered the stones after the earthquake. The punishment inflicted
upon the tyrants and warmakers is clearly related to their faults: because

they were bloodthirsty during their lives, they are now condemned to stay in Phlegethon, the river of boiling blood, forever. The motif of the damned gradually immersed in a river—usually of fire—was commonplace in the medieval representation of Hell.

Though Dante usually personifies the particular sin he is discussing, in the first round of the seventh circle, which is the place of punishment for those who have been violent against their neighbors, Dante does not single out any one person. He is content to merely mention the names of various tyrants and violent warriors, particularly those who belong to the Ghibelline party, as though his readers would well understand the meaning behind the names.

The minotaur and the centaurs are much like their figures in mythology. The minotaur is violent and bloodthirsty, a fitting guardian for this seventh circle. The centaurs, half-man and half-horse, were, in mythology, creatures of sudden violence, though the wise Chiron was the legendary teacher of Achilles, Theseus, and other great heroes.

These figures, along with the Harpies in the next canto, are grotesque combinations of human and beast, and are symbolic of the transition from the sins of incontinence in the higher circles to the sins of bestiality in the very pit of Hell.

CANTO 13

Summary

Dante and Virgil enter a wood where there is no path. This is a dismal wood of strange black leaves, misshapen branches, and poison sticks instead of fruit: it is the place where the Harpies nest.

Virgil explains that this is the second round of the seventh circle, where Dante will see things that will cause him to doubt Virgil's words. Dante has already heard cries, but cannot find where they come from and in confusion stops where he is. He believes that Virgil knows his thoughts: the spirits making such an outcry are hiding among the trees. Virgil tells him only to break off any branch, and he will see that he is mistaken in his thought.

Dante pulls a small branch from a large thorn tree, and a voice asks why Dante tears at him. Blood comes from the tree, and with it the voice which asks if Dante has no pity. It continues, saying that all these trees were once men and that Dante should have mercy upon them. Dante drops the branch, and Virgil tells the tree-spirit that if Dante had believed what Virgil had once written, this would not have happened. Since Dante could not believe, Virgil had asked him to pull off the branch, though it grieved Virgil to wound the spirit.

In compensation for this wound, Virgil asks the spirit to tell Dante his story, so that he may repeat it when he returns to earth. The spirit, moved by his words, tells his story: he was minister to Frederick II and absolutely faithful to him, but the envy of the court turned Frederick against him. Because he could not bear to lose this trust, in sorrow he killed himself. He swears he was faithful to the end and asks that Dante tell the true story when he returns to the upper world.

Virgil tells Dante to question the spirit if he wishes, but Dante is too sorrowful and asks Virgil to say the things Dante wishes to know. Virgil therefore asks how the souls are bound into these gnarled trees and if any ever regains freedom.

The imprisoned spirit replies that when the soul is torn from the body (by suicide), it is sent by Minos to the seventh circle, where it falls to the ground, sprouts, and grows. The Harpies eat its leaves, giving it great pain. The spirits will all be called to the Last Judgment, and will reclaim the mortal bodies forsaken by them but will never regain the immortal souls which they took from themselves and will remain forever trapped in this strange wood.

The two poets now hear a noise like a hunt crashing through a forest, and two spirits appear. The second flings himself into a bush, but is quickly caught and torn apart by the pursuing hounds, who carry him off.

Dante and Virgil approach the bush, which is complaining loudly that the fleeing spirit gained nothing by choosing it for a hiding place. Virgil asks this spirit who he was, but in answering, it first asks that they gather up all the leaves which have been torn off in the hunt, then says only that he was a citizen of Florence, who hanged himself in his own house.

Commentary

The meaning of the punishment of the suicides is evident: those who on earth deprived themselves of their bodies, in Hell are deprived of a human form. At the Last Judgment the suicides will rise, like all the other souls, to claim their bodies, but will never wear them. Their bodies will remain suspended on the trees which enclose the spirits of their owners.

One of the greatest changes brought on by the advent of Christianity is the change that took place in judging the suicide. In classical times, when a person could no longer live in freedom, or when he could no longer live heroically, it was considered a stoic virtue for him to die by his own hand. The last great act that a person could perform was to take his own life, which was for him the last free choice he could make.

With the coming of Christianity, however, Jesus preached the concept that a man is free inwardly and no amount of imprisonment, no amount of disgrace could destroy one's spiritual attributes. Thus, where suicide was a virtue in the ancient days, for the Christian it became one of the cardinal sins.

Dante is (naturally) very confused when he arrives at the wood of suicides and hears human sounds but sees no human forms. Consequently Virgil has to do something which seems extremely cruel. He has Dante pick off a branch from one of the trees, which causes the tree to bleed. We have seen before that Dante is a person of infinite pity; therefore the words of the tree evoke from us the expected response — surprise and sympathy.

The entire scene becomes a fantasy as Dante breaks the branch, the tree bleeds, and a voice comes from the tree. It seems almost as though Dante is unconscious of the words; instead it is the startling *fact* that a tree speaks that evokes his feeling of awe and disbelief.

The story of Pier delle Vigne is related so that Dante, on his return to earth, can justify the man's loyalty (though not his suicide). The greatness of the episode comes when Pier delle Vigne says that in order to make himself a just individual, by one stroke of the knife he has made himself forever unjust. Here is a gentleman, a man of honesty, elegance, and breeding, a cultured and intellectual man, who has condemned himself forever to damnation by a single act.

This is one of the great poetic concepts in the *Inferno*. The spirit is not seen as a mean or evil or vicious man; instead he is a man who, in a moment of weakness, has taken his own life. Most of the other characters that we meet in Hell have something despicable about them, but Pier delle Vigne rouses our sympathy in that a man of his obvious greatness should, in a moment of weakness of will, take the irretrievable action, and after a life of service and devotion, be condemned forever.

The naked men pursued and torn to pieces by hounds are spendthrifts, reckless squanderers, who did not actually take their own lives but destroyed themselves by destroying the means of life. The difference between these sinners and the spendthrifts of the fourth circle is that the earlier cases arise from weakness, these later cases from an act of will.

The Harpies were winged creatures with the faces of women and were symbolic of the whirlwind or the violent storm. They stole anything; hence in the wood they symbolize the violence of the suicide and the stealing away of his soul.

CANTO 14

Summary

Dante gathers the leaves and returns them to the bush, and the poets pass to the other edge of the wood. Here is the beginning of a desolate plain, and Dante looks fearfully about him. Many souls are on this plain, some lying down, some crouching, some wandering restlessly. Flakes of fire fall on this desert, making it burn and increasing the pain of these spirits who were violent against God. They try to save themselves from the rain of fire by waving it away with their hands.

Dante's attention turns to one spirit who lies on the sand without moving, paying no attention to the falling flakes. Dante asks Virgil his name, but the spirit himself answers that he is the same dead as he was living (that is, unconquered and blasphemous), and that even if Zeus has thunderbolts to hurl forever, he will never succeed in subduing this shade. This is Capaneus, killed by a thunderbolt from the hand of the angry Zeus. Virgil calls him by name and upbraids him for his pride, in a tone that Dante has never heard him use before.

Virgil tells Dante that this is the spirit of one of the Seven against Thebes, and that for his defiance of the gods, he is confined here.

Virgil asks Dante to follow and not step on the burning sand but stay close to the wood. Walking between the two rounds, they reach a small stream which is so red it disgusts Dante. Its banks are stone, and it quenches the fire even in the desert near it; Dante realizes that this is the path they must follow across the burning sand. Virgil tells him this is the most remarkable thing they have yet seen, and Dante asks him to explain.

His guide begins a long discourse. The island of Crete, he says, was ruled by a great king in the Golden Age. On the island is Mount Ida, once green with trees but now arid. This is the very mountain on which the goddess Rhea, wife of the jealous Cronus, had hidden her son to save him and ordered great noise to be made so the king could not hear his cries. Inside the mountain is a strange and wonderful being, who stands with his shoulders toward Damietta (Egypt), his face toward Rome. His head is made of gold, his arms and chest of silver; his torso is brass, and his legs of iron, except that his right foot is of clay, and he puts more weight upon this foot.

Except for his head, every part of his body has cracks from which tears come forth. These collect in the cavern where he stands, then run down into Hell, forming Acheron, Styx, and Phlegethon; this stream which they now follow; and, at the bottom where it can flow no farther, Cocytus, whose nature Dante will later see for himself.

Dante then asks his master a question: if the stream has flowed such a distance — from Crete to the center of the earth — why are they seeing it only now? Virgil answers that in descending the abyss, which is circular, they have been bearing to the left and have therefore not made a complete circle. If Dante sees new and strange things, this is the reason.

Again Dante has a question. Where can Phlegethon and Lethe be found? Virgil is pleased by this interest, and points out that the boiling red stream (Phlegethon) has already been passed, but that Lethe is not part of this abyss, and flows in another place, where the spirits who have been doing penance may then wash themselves.

The poets leave the wood, and Dante is warned to follow the edge of the stream closely to avoid the fire of the burning desert.

Commentary

The intellectual concept of Capaneus in Canto 14 is one of the great characterizations in the *Inferno*. The character of Capaneus re-emphasizes one concept of Dante's Hell, that is, that the person retains those very qualities which sent him to Hell. In classical times, Capaneus was a figure who thought himself so strong that not even Jove (Zeus, or Jupiter) could destroy him, but he *was* destroyed by the thunderbolts of Jove. For his blasphemy on earth he is condemned to Hell, and his first words to Dante are "Such as I was alive, such am I also in death." This emphasizes that he has *not* changed.

Although Virgil does upbraid Capaneus for his pride, Dante seems to be drawn toward this powerful figure who dared to defy the gods. For example, look at the difference in character between Capaneus and Fucci (Cantos 24-25), who "made figs" at God and blasphemed him. There is a certain power in Capaneus' defiance (certainly lacking in Fucci!), and even in Hell he remains as he was on earth—and has the blind strength to say so. Being condemned to death because of his pride and his blasphemy, in Hell he remains filled with pride and continues to blaspheme against God. Capaneus insults God even yet by saying that Jove himself will grow weary of trying to punish him before he, Capaneus, will give in to Jove's punishment. This is the ultimate defiance.

We have expressed here an idea which is important throughout Hell: that in any particular circle the *degree* of punishment is not always the same. Capaneus is being punished more than anyone else in this circle and, according to Virgil, as Capaneus keeps blaspheming against God, his punishment will increase throughout eternity.

There occurs in the canto one of the longest passages concerning a mythological being. This is the Old Man of Crete, whose flawed figure is symbolic of the imperfect ages of mankind—save for the perfect golden head which is the sign of the golden age. From the flaws come the tears which are the sorrows of man, flowing through Hell and depositing all the filth of sin at the feet of Satan.

Dante apparently makes an error of recollection in this canto. Virgil describes the course of the repulsive little red stream, naming the rivers it has formed as it flowed downward. Dante asks (lines 121-22) why they have not seen it before if it has flowed the long distance from Crete. The point is, of course, that they *have* seen it before, and Dante already knew the names of both the river Acheron and the marsh of Styx (which Virgil has just repeated) and has crossed Phlegethon, although he did not know its

48

name. (Reference to Lethe will be found in the last canto and in the *Purgatorio*.)

CANTO 15

Summary

Dante and Virgil follow the stone bank of the river, which Dante compares to a dike holding back the sea. They walk a long distance across the burning plain, and can no longer see the wood, when they meet a group of spirits. These spirits peer at the two poets as though in darkness, until one of them recognizes Dante and speaks to him.

Dante looks at the spirit's face, so terribly changed by the searing heat, and calls him by name: Ser Brunetto. Brunetto asks if he may walk with them, and Dante of course is delighted to have him, asking if he wishes to sit down and talk. Brunetto explains that whoever stops for an instant must spend a hundred years without fanning himself in the terrible heat. He will walk beside Dante, talking as they go. And so, with Brunetto walking on the plain and Dante on the bank, they continue their journey.

Brunetto asks why Dante has come here and who his guide is. Dante tells the story of his first adventure on the mountain and his rescue by Virgil, though he does not give his name. Brunetto, in symbolic language, foretells the future fame of Dante, a fame which Brunetto would gladly have aided if he had lived. He also prophesies the events of Dante's exile.

Dante speaks with great kindness and gratitude for Brunetto's past help and teaching, and tells him that he thinks of him often. Dante also says he will ask a certain lady about the prophecies and is prepared to accept what Fortune wills for him. Virgil glances back and tells Dante that he is right to listen and remember.

Dante asks Brunetto who is with him on the burning plain, and is told that only a few can be mentioned, since time is short. All the spirits with him were scholars of renown and all are guilty of the same crime (sodomy, though Brunetto does not name it). He sees a new group approaching and he is not allowed to be with them; therefore he recommends his great book, the *Tresor*, to Dante and runs off.

Commentary

Dante meets the spirit of the man who did so much to guide and encourage his work. This was the illustrious scholar, Ser Brunetto Latini, whom Dante finds in the circle of sodomites. Their meeting is full of sorrow, and Dante greets Brunetto with love and deference, addressing him with the plural *you* as a sign of respect.

The meeting and conversation with Latini is one of the high points of the *Inferno*. Even Dante's posture while walking, though imposed by the conditions of their miserable surroundings, reveals the reverence he felt for this great master.

Brunetto gives Dante some fatherly advice about his future and expresses his wish to help, which no doubt he could have done, had he lived, for he was an important man in his time. He also warns Dante against the political division of Florence (which had already happened, of course).

Brunetto Latini was one who understood Dante's genius when others failed to do so; now the poet still finds in his master the support and the encouragement he needs to withstand the attacks that his fellow citizens are going to direct at him. In Brunetto Latini, Dante finds a sympathetic echo of his own disdain and pride. By his master Dante is encouraged to follow his star in order not to miss the glorious fortune for which he is destined.

The exchange of sentiments between the young and the old man is touching and compelling; if Ser Brunetto understands Dante so well, so does the poet understand his master when Brunetto recommends his *Tresor (Li Livres dou Tresor)*, hoping that the fame of his great encyclopedic work is still alive in the world.

Dante's tribute to Brunetto is a sincere and moving one. Brunetto was not Dante's teacher in the formal sense, but rather his adviser, who took an interest in Dante, fostered his intellectual development, and served as his inspiration.

The symbolism of the rain of fire and the scorching sand is that of sterility and unproductiveness: the rain should be life-giving, the soil fertile. Instead, symbolically the sex practice of the sodomite is unnatural in that it is not life-giving; the practice of the usurer is unnatural because it is unproductive of anything except more money — a contemptible act in Dante's time.

CANTOS 16-17

Summary

Dante can hear the waterfall ahead, where the stream falls into the next lower circle, but before they reach it, the two poets see three spirits leave a large group and come toward them. The spirits recognize the distinctive Florentine dress (a long gown and folded hood) which Dante wears, and they ask him to wait. Dante is saddened by their wounds, which have been caused by the flakes of fire.

As the spirits approach, Virgil says that these are ones who deserve courtesy. The spirits again are crying out, and as they reach the two poets, they start walking in a circle (for, as Brunetto said, they dare not stop), and telling their stories.

One says they should not be looked upon with contempt because of their present condition, for in life they were famous. They wish to know what a living man is doing in Hell. Before Dante can answer, the spirit continues. The one ahead of him is Guido Guerra, a famous commander, and behind him is Tegghiaio Aldobrandi, a counselor of Guerra. The speaker is Jacopo Rusticucci, whose reputation has been greatly harmed by his own wife.

Dante would have embraced these three, leaders of his own party, but the fire prevents it. He can only tell them that he is indeed a Florentine (as his dress has shown) and that he will not forget their sorrow. He has heard and spoken of their great deeds all his life. He will be leaving Hell behind, but first he must visit the lower circles.

The spirits wish him long life and fame, and ask if Florence is still the same fine city they left, for another spirit lately arrived has told them otherwise. Sorrowfully Dante tells them that Florence is now a proud and sinful city. The spirits ask him to speak of them when he returns to earth, and then run to join their group.

Dante and Virgil have now come so close to the waterfall they can hardly hear each other. Dante has a cord tied around his waist—he had hoped to catch the leopard with it earlier—and Virgil asks him to untie it. Dante hands it to him in a coil, and he flings it far out into the abyss. Dante realizes this is some kind of signal, and Virgil tells him that what he expects will soon be there.

Knowing what what he is about to tell will scarcely be believed, Dante swears it is true: that such a creature as he had never dreamed of came swimming up through the darkness of the pit.

Virgil tells Dante that this wild beast with the pointed tail can go over mountains and destroy walls and weapons; he is the beast that corrupts the world.

Dante sees the figure of Fraud: the pleasant and kindly face of a man, hairy paws and arms, and the body of a snake painted in designs such as Dante has never seen before. It rests its arms upon the edge of the pit, showing only its head and shoulders and the end of its poisonous tail.

Virgil says they must go to him, and they step down onto an empty space which is not burning and see another group of spirits sitting. Virgil directs Dante to talk with them while he persuades the beast to carry them, and Dante walks toward the weeping spirits. They sit on the very edge of the circle, trying to brush off the flakes of fire, and Dante sees that each of them has a crested pouch hanging from his neck. Each spirit looks unmoving at his own pouch, and each crest is different. These are the usurers.

One spirit speaks to Dante, ordering him to leave because he is alive. The spirit continues to talk, however, and tells Dante that Vitaliano shall soon sit on the plain beside him. He is the only Paduan; the rest are of Florence, and they often cry out the name of another Florentine who will soon join them. The spirit sticks out his tongue at Dante, who retreats quickly, to find Virgil already on the back of the monster. Virgil orders him to mount quickly; Dante turns pale but obeys. Virgil holds him and orders the monster Geryon to circle slowly to their landing place.

Dante is terrified by the descent and can see nothing, though he can feel the strong wind and hear the whirlpool below. Finally, he gathers courage and looks down, but the sight and sound are frightening: he sees fires and hears great cries. Geryon sets them down near the bottom of the jagged rocks and flies off like an arrow.

Commentary

Canto 16 holds less interest in comparison to the sincerity and sorrow of the preceding canto. The allusions here are almost entirely political.

Dante's answer to the three Florentines represents his own diagnosis of the swift changes which actually took place in Florence at the end of the thirteenth century because of a rapid transformation in the economy and in the society of the commune. Dante sees in these economic and social changes the origin of the moral decadence of the city and the cause for the disappearance of the old habits that were dear to him. His words hold disdain for the "upstart people" and distrust for the new fashions which he does not understand and, therefore, does not like. The same feelings are expressed repeatedly in the *Divine Comedy*.

The description of the usurers, who try to defend themselves from the rain of fire and the hot soil, is full of contempt and is intended to stress the degradation of those men of noble stock who were in fact ignoble and contemptible. Their faces, scorched as they are by the flakes of fire, have lost all human aspect and are not recognizable; their movements are not those of men, but of animals. All their humanity has been consumed by their thirst for gold; therefore the only signs which distinguish one from the other are the moneybags, which hang from their necks. They are disgusting and despicable in Dante's eyes.

Much of the critical interest in this canto centers on the symbolism of the cord which Dante wears and which Virgil tosses into the pit as a signal. It is believed that the cord may have some connection with the Franciscan order, in which it symbolizes humility. By Dante's own admission he had hoped to catch the leopard with it. If the leopard symbolized incontinence, Dante may be indicating that he had hoped to overcome his errors (pride in his work or perhaps too great a dependence on philosophy?) through humility. This is only one of many interpretations. Whatever the significance of the cord, it serves as a command to the monster which personifies fraud.

The monster Geryon has a kindly face, but the decorations of his body symbolize the twisted dealings of the fraudulent. The scorpion's tail is symbolic of the *coup de grâce* which completes the fraud, the unexpected sting from one who proves unworthy of trust.

Dante has described admirably the swimming motions of Geryon, which carry him like an eel through the dark air, but the clearest image is that of the falcon, deprived of his prey, who wheels and sinks in flight, sullenly ignoring his master. In contrast, when Geryon is relieved of the burden of Dante's weight, the monstrous figure is airborne in an instant.

CANTOS 18-19

Summary

Dante describes Malebolge, the eighth circle, in which increasingly terrible sins are punished. Its walls are made of stone, and exactly in the center is a well which Dante says he will describe later.

Malebolge is round, as the other levels have been, but it is divided into ten deep, concentric valleys, whose banks go down like stairsteps toward the central well. Across these valleys, going from bank to bank, are bridges which lead to the well.

Dante and his guide move away from the place where Geryon has left them and start toward the left. They see the first chasm, or valley, filled with tormented sinners walking in both directions. Demons with horns flog them continuously to keep them moving.

One of the shades looks up at Dante, who recognizes him. Dante goes back a few steps, and although the spirit tries to hide his face, Dante calls him by name. It is Venedico Caccianimico, and the spirit is compelled to tell Dante his ugly story: the spirit arranged the seduction of his own sister Ghisola. As if in his own defense, he says he is not the only one from Bologna in this circle of panderers. A demon strikes him with a whip and orders him on.

Dante rejoins Virgil, and they start across the bridge on the first chasm. They stop in the middle to look down at the circle of sinners going in the direction opposite from the panderers. The first figure they see is that of the proud Jason, who gives no sign of pain; with him are other seducers.

The two cross to the bank of the second chasm and, because they cannot see the bottom, again go to the middle of the bridge. This is the circle of flatterers, whose shades are sunk in excrement.

Dante sees someone he knows, Alessio Interminei of Lucca, who says he is sunk to the top of his head because his tongue could never stop its flattery. Virgil directs Dante to look farther on, at the figure of a woman. He identifies her as Thais, who flattered her lover extravagantly when he sent her a gift. With this, the two poets have seen enough.

Dante now speaks out against those of the third chasm, the simonists, who trade the grace and favor of the church for money. Standing in the middle of the bridge, Dante sees that the bottom of the chasm is full of round holes. From each of these holes protrude the feet and legs of a spirit, with the rest of his body upside down in the hole. The soles of their feet are on fire, and Dante sees one shade who is apparently suffering more torment than others, moving and shaking, his feet burning more fiercely than any others.

Naturally Dante wishes to know who it is, and Virgil replies that if Dante will go with him, he will find out. They descend to the bottom of the chasm and stand next to the pit of the sinner. Dante asks him to speak, if he can; the spirit replies by calling him Boniface and asking if he is here already, before his time.

Startled, Dante cannot answer until Virgil tells him to say simply that he is not Boniface, which he does. The spirit weeps and tells Dante that since he was so curious to know the shade's identity, he will tell him: he was a pope (Nicholas III) who engaged in simony. Below him, in cracks in the rock, are other popes who did the same. When the next pope shall join them, Nicholas, too, will fall down into the stone.

Dante reproaches the shade by asking him how much gold Jesus asked of Peter before he gave him the keys of the kingdom and reminding him that the only requirement was that Peter should follow Jesus. And, he says, Peter and the other disciples asked for no money when they chose Matthias to take the place of Judas. The poet can barely restrain his words; he believes these sinners are receiving the punishment they deserve, and only his respect for the former high office they held keeps him from saying worse things. As it is, he continues his tirade, observing that Virgil is pleased.

At last Virgil picks him up, climbs the side of the chasm, and walks to the center of the next bridge, where Dante sees another valley below him.

Commentary

The poets have entered the circle of Malebolge. There is a certain amount of confusion over the terminology, which can lead to a confusion of images. The word "bolgia" in Italian means both "pit" and "pouch," but neither term seems to be the best translation for the idea Dante wanted to convey. The words "chasm" or "ravine" seem to carry the connotation of depth and ruggedness that Dante would wish, but "moat" would probably be equally acceptable, as Dante implies in an early stanza. The word "well" might be replaced with "crater" or "abyss" in the interests of clarity.

Malebolge is a terrible place, in the real sense of the word. Dante has devoted thirteen cantos to this one circle of Hell. These are the heart of the *Inferno* and contain some of the most dramatic scenes, both in content and in poetic richness. Canto 18 opens with a long descriptive passage unequalled in the *inferno*.

Dante seems to be drawn to the figures of courageous heroes. Here Jason is described as undaunted by his punishment; earlier the proud

Capaneus captured the imagination of Dante, as will the figure of Ulysses later.

The opening lines of Canto 19 are a bitter denunciation of the simonists, reflecting Dante's preoccupation with the corruption of his church. The sinners are punished in a manner which is a curious reversal of baptismal practices of the time: they are plunged head down in narrow pits and are tortured by fire playing on the soles of their feet, rather than being cleansed and purified by the cool sweetness of holy water.

Dante describes the pits and takes the opportunity to refute publicly a charge (probably of sacrilege) brought against him years earlier. He had broken the baptismal font at San Giovanni, he says, in order to save someone from drowning.

The subject of simony seems to rouse Dante to rage, as any corrupt practice of the church did. It also elevates him to the heights of poetic expression, as he angrily demands an answer to his questions, and he sternly rebukes Pope Nicholas even as he reiterates his reverence for the papal office.

CANTO 20

Summary

Dante views the shades who are walking slowly and weeping. He is amazed to discover that their heads are turned backward on their bodies. They are not simply looking over their shoulders; their heads have been turned around so that they are forced to walk backward in order to see where they are going, and as they weep their tears run down their backs. Dante weeps to see such distortion of the human body.

Virgil reproves him for questioning the judgment of God on the sinners and tells him to look at the shades. They are ones who sinned by trying to foretell the future, which is known only to God. He names several, ending the list with the name of Manto the sorceress, mythical founder of the city of Mantua, Virgil's birthplace. He tells the long story of the founding of the city and asks Dante to promise that, if he ever hears any other version, he will tell this, the true story. Dante promises and asks Virgil to point out more of the spirits by name.

Virgil indicates Eurypylus, who, with Calchas, determined by sorcery the propitious time for the Greek ships to set sail against Troy. Virgil says that Dante surely must remember the story from Virgil's own writings. He then points out Michael Scott, a writer on the occult sciences; Guido Bonatti (an astrologer); and Asdente, who had been a shoemaker before he turned to sorcery. These are followed by many women who left their proper work to become witches.

Virgil urges Dante to hurry on, for the moon is already setting. Virgil reminds Dante that the moon was full and lighted his way while he wandered in the dark wood; then they walk on toward the next circle.

Commentary

There is a definite break in the narrative here. Dante the writer intrudes upon Dante the pilgrim; once before, in Canto 16, he has mentioned his writing, but it was less obtrusive. Then he simply said "I swear by this my Comedy."

If Dante was in the habit of sending several finished cantos to Can Grande della Scala, perhaps Canto 19 marks the end of one of those sections and Canto 20 the beginning of another. There may have been a lapse of time, during which Can Grande read and returned previous cantos, with his comments.

Dante, following the teachings of the church, obviously did not approve of sorcery in any form, and therefore would seek to negate Virgil's reputation as a white magician. In his long discourse on the origins of his native city of Mantua, Virgil denies that its founding was in any way attributed to the influence of Manto, the sorceress. By this devious means Dante seeks to clear Virgil of guilt by association, emphatically declaring that this and only this is the true story of the founding of Mantua.

For the first time, Dante violates his own concept of judging each spirit by the standards of the time in which it lived. Here he condemns the Greek prophets, who were held in high esteem in their own time. One would think Dante would also be forced then to condemn the prophets of the Old Testament, and since he is silent on this point, it is difficult to see the fine line of distinction drawn by Dante. His only argument could be that the gift of prophecy, or the genuine spirit of prophecy, was valid only as a forerunner of Christianity, hence offering, in effect, another excuse for Virgil.

Though he does not approve, Dante can still sympathize with the plight of the sinners and their torment which makes them appear less than human. In life these spirits tried to look ahead into the future; now they are condemned to look behind them. Considering this condemnation, why are all the spirits of Hell given the power to foresee the future? Is it because the knowledge of events and disasters of future times will increase their torments?

CANTOS 21-23

Summary

The travelers cross to the center of the next bridge and view the next chasm, which is extremely dark. Dante compares it with the arsenal in Venice where pitch is boiled to caulk the ships and other repairs are made.

This is indeed a river of boiling pitch, which has splashed up on the banks everywhere. Dante can see nothing except bubbles and some indication of movement beneath its surface. He leans over to look more closely, but Virgil warns him to be careful, not of the bridge, but of another danger. Dante turns to see a black demon approach, carrying a new spirit over his shoulders. He calls to the Malebranche (Evil Claws) of the bridge to push this citizen of Lucca (the city of Saint Zita) under the pitch, while he goes back to the same city for more, for there is a plentiful supply there. He throws the spirit into the circle of barrators, or grafters—those who profit from their position in public office—and hastens back for more.

The shade is tossed into the pitch and comes to the surface, but the demons under the bridge warn him that the will not swim here as he did in the river Serchio, near Lucca. He must stay under the surface or be punished with their hooks, and they strike him to make him plunge downward. Whatever he may steal, they say, he will take in secret, as he did in life.

Virgil now orders Dante to hide himself in the ruins of the bridge and to remain silent no matter what happens, since Virgil has been this way before and can handle matters himself.

Virgil walks calmly to the bank of the sixth chasm. All of the demons of the bridge rush at him, threatening him with their weapons, but Virgil holds them off momentarily by asking to talk with one of their number. Malacoda (Evil Tail) comes forward, asking what good this conference will do.

Virgil tells him firmly that he and Dante are safe from any harm, since their journey was willed in Heaven. Malecoda drops his hook and orders the others not to attack. Virgil then calls to Dante, in somewhat unflattering terms, and tells him to come forward. Dante goes to his side and stands close, fearing that the demons, who have moved closer, may not follow the orders of Malacoda.

The demons do not raise their hooks to threaten Dante, but instead taunt him by talking among themselves, suggesting that he should be tormented with their hooks—just a little.

Malacoda silences them roughly, then turns to Virgil and tells him that the nearest bridge across the sixth chasm is broken (and he gives the exact date and hour when it happened) but that there is another bridge not far ahead. Some of his men (demons) are going to walk along the bank to keep the spirits under the pitch, and the two poets can accompany them in safety. He calls a patrol of ten demons forward, ordering to watch for rebellious shades. He tells them that the two travelers will go with them as far as the unbroken bridge.

Dante is terrified at going with these demons and asks Virgil if they cannot find the way alone. He points out the demons, frowning and gnashing their teeth, but Virgil says this show of fierceness is for the spirits not for them.

The patrol marches away, along the bank, each saluting the captain by sticking out his tongue, and the captain replies by breaking wind with a noise like a trumpet.

Dante is a man of considerable military experience, but he has never before experienced an exchange of salutes like this one! Still shaken by the presence of the demons, he accepts it more or less philosophically, and the two poets follow the demons.

Dante's interest now is not in the demons but in the luckless sinners trapped in the mess of pitch. Occasionally one will rise to the surface like a dolphin and as quickly disappear; others sit near the bank, submerged like frogs with only their muzzles showing. All but one disappear as the demon Barbariccia approaches, and this one is hooked like an otter by the demon Graffiacane and dragged up out of the pitch.

As the demons call out, Dante, who has remembered the name of each one, listens as they shout to Rubicante to claw this sinner and flog him well. Dante asks his master to learn the name and story of this shade. Virgil moves closer, and in reply to his question, the spirit answers that he is from Navarre and was in the service of King Thibaut. He used his position to sell political favors, and that is why he is being tortured here.

As he is speaking, the demon Ciriatto rips at him with one of his long tusks; Barbariccia, who is holding the shade, orders the demons back, then turns to Virgil and tells him to go on with his questions before another demon attacks. Virgil asks if any Latian lies below. The shade replies that he has just now seen one from the other side (Sardinia) and wishes he were down with him now.

Another demon attacks, hooking his arm, and a second tries to jab his legs, but their leader quells them with a look – temporarily. Virgil asks the name of this barrator from Sardinia, and the shade replies that it is Friar Gomita of Gallura, who worked so smoothly he was indeed a king among barrators. Don Michel Zanche is with him, and they never tire of talking about Sardinia.

Another demon threatens and is warned off. The shade offers to call more spirits, these from Tuscany and Lombardy, if the demons can be kept back. One of the demons instantly suspects a trick, which the shade denies, and a second demon threatens the spirit, saying that if he tries to escape, the demon will not run after him but will fly to the very surface of the pitch to catch him.

The demons are beginning to quarrel among themselves when the spirit sees his chance, dives into the pitch, and goes under. Two demons start after him, one pulling up in his flight just before he reaches the river of pitch, the second attacking him because he has let the sinner escape. Like two birds of prey they battle with their claws, only to become mired in the pitch so they cannot fly. The captain sends four more demons to rescue them with their hooks, and Dante and Virgil leave the noisy scene of the quarrel.

The two poets walk in welcome silence, and Dante is lost in thought, recalling Aesop's fable of the frog and the mouse, in which the frog offers to tie the mouse to his leg and carry him over a marsh but dives into the water, drowning the mouse; a hawk then carries off both of them. Following this train of thought, Dante recalls the demons, who may blame the two poets for the whole quarrel, and adding anger to their natural evil, may pursue the travelers.

By now he is thoroughly frightened and begs Virgil to hide them quickly. Virgil has had the same thought and has already decided to climb down into the next chasm. The demons are in fact pursuing them, and Virgil picks Dante up, as a mother would a child, and carries him rapidly to the very bottom of the seventh chasm. This leaves the demons high above them on the bank in impotent rage, for these pursuers can no more leave their own realm than the condemned sinners can.

The travelers see that the chasm is filled with spirits walking very slowly, as with a heavy burden. These shades wear cloaks and hoods that are dazzling with their glitter but lined with lead. Dante and Virgil turn to the left and follow the bed of the chasm but are walking faster than the spirits, so Dante asks Virgil to find someone they might know.

A spirit calls to Dante, recognizing his Tuscan speech, and asks him to wait. Two spirits approach without speaking. Finally one observes that Dante must be alive because his throat moves. Speaking to Dante, they ask why he has come to this valley of hypocrites and who he is.

Dante says he is a Florentine and is indeed alive; in turn, he asks who they are who weep so bitterly and what their punishment is. The answer is given: their bright cloaks are of thick lead and their punishment is to carry them forever. They were of the order of the Jovial Friars and had been named to govern Florence jointly, in order to keep the peace.

Dante angrily begins to speak to the friars of their evil, when he sees a figure on the ground held by three stakes. Friar Catalano explains that this is one (Caiaphas, the high priest) who told the Council that it was better for Jesus to die than for the whole nation to perish. Therefore he lies where each one who passes must step upon him, and his father-in-law (Annas) and all the Council are punished in the same manner. Virgil looks at Caiaphas for some time. Finally he turns and asks the friar if there is a bridge over the chasm. The friar answers that all were destroyed at the same time, but the travelers may climb out on the ruins of one nearby without much difficulty.

Virgil realizes that Malacoda has lied to him about the bridges, as he had about the dependability of the bodyguard. Angrily he walks away from the cloaked spirits, and Dante follows.

Commentary

The opening lines of Canto 21 probably refer to a further discussion between the two poets concerning witchcraft and sorcery. Dante does not care to repeat the conversation, first, because it is not a proper topic for his *Comedy,* and second, because he probably does not wish for any further reflection on Virgil as a white magician.

All three cantos are bright with imagery and description, and lack any trace of that moral concern which is inspired by other scenes of torment. Dante compares the chasm with the arsenal at Venice; he describes the demons and their tortures with gusto, making them seem a bunch of fiendish rascals gleefully applying their hooks. There is not the somber tone of many other cantos, and when Virgil discovers that Malacoda has told two outright lies, he stalks across the floor of the chasm in a very human manner. The flow of the narrative and the poetic unity to the end of the cantos show Dante's art at its best.

The destruction of the bridges, as well as the landslide Virgil has described, was believed to have taken place when Jesus was crucified and an earthquake occurred. (See Canto 12.) One wonders, though, why Caiaphas, who presided at the Council that sentenced Jesus to death, is not in the circle of evil counselors.

Virgil is something less than sympathetic to Dante. Having ordered Dante to hide in the ruins of the bridge, he calls him forth with a suggestion of rebuke for cowering among the stones.

In the circle of hypocrites, Dante is again recognized as being alive, this time because his throat moves as he talks. The cloaks of the hypocrites, which dazzle the eye, actually are instruments of torture. Moreover, the heavy garments they wear force the sinners to adopt a decorous and subdued attitude which is entirely in character with their worldly habit of hiding a vicious nature beneath a virtuous and holy appearance.

Dante has placed the hypocrites far down in the circles of Hell. Their presence is a restatement of Dante's definition of sin as perversion of the intellect; few sins can equal the deliberate cloaking of one's true character and feelings in a false aspect of piety, tolerance, or honesty.

CANTOS 24-25

Summary

Virgil's anger, though not directed at him, has made Dante as downcast and troubled as a shepherd without pasture for his sheep. Dante is dependent upon his master not only for physical help but also for spiritual guidance and moral support, and it now seems to Dante that this has been withdrawn with alarming suddenness. One look from Virgil soon calms his spirit, however, for he wears the same benign expression as when Dante first saw him.

Virgil's plan is clear: he has looked at the ruins of the bridge and knows it can be climbed if they are careful. The ascent presents no problem for Virgil—he is weightless—but he gives careful directions to Dante to test each rock before he puts his weight on it. Holding (and pushing) Dante from behind, Virgil selects the route and they mount from rock to rock. Dante is well aware that, even if Virgil could have climbed it alone, he himself could not have done it without help.

At last they reach the top, and Dante drops exhausted. Virgil somewhat unfeelingly urges him forward, saying he cannot gain the heights if he is lazy. Dante pretends that he has overcome his exhaustion and with false eagerness goes ahead, talking all the time as if he were not out of breath. A voice from the chasm answers; Dante cannot make out the words even though they are now in the middle of the bridge, but the voice speaks in anger.

Dante can see nothing in the darkness of the seventh chasm and tells his master so. They walk to the end of the bridge, where it rests on the wall between the seventh and eighth chasms, and look down on the mass of strange serpents below them. Even the memory of this makes Dante's blood run cold.

The poets see naked people running, with no place to hide, nor, as Dante says, with any hope of invisibility (the heliotrope was a stone supposed to make its wearer invisible). There are strange and terrifying sights: the hands of each shade are tied behind him with a serpent, whose head and tail are thrust through the spirit's body at the loins and tied in coils and knots at the front; another serpent sinks its fangs in the neck of a shade, who immediately takes fire and burns to ashes on the ground, only to resume its shape—and its torment—once again. This shade seems bewildered by what has happened, as one who has been the victim of a seizure of some kind.

Virgil asks who he is, and he answers that he came recently from Tuscany, where he lived the life of a beast. He gives his name as Vanni Fucci of Pistoia. Dante asks what his crime was, for he had seen him once and considered him a man of violence. The spirit, ashamed, confesses that it hurts him more for Dante to see him there than it did to be condemned for his sin. He had robbed the sacristy of a church (San Zeno), and although his crime had gone undetected for a time, he was condemned to this chasm of thieves. He then prophesies, in somewhat obscure language, a future battle involving Pistoia first, then Florence itself, and Dante's party shall suffer greatly from it.

Dante is shocked by the next action of the thief, who makes an obscene gesture with both hands, and shouts blasphemies in the face of God. Dante is gratified when one of the serpents coils around the thief's neck, silencing him, and another binds his arms to his sides. Dante laments the evil of the citizens of Pistoia, saying that in all of Hell he has seen no spirit so blasphemous, not even Capaneus. The shade runs off, and is immediately followed by a monster (mistakenly called a centaur by Dante) who is covered with snakes up to his waist and bears a firebreathing dragon on his back.

Virgil identifies this creature as Cacus, who stole some of Hercules' cattle, for which Hercules killed him with his club. The monster runs off, and Dante and Virgil hear the voices of three shades asking who the travelers are. Dante does not know them but learns their names as they call to one another.

In the most vivid language, Dante tells of the two horrible transformations that take place. One of the shades is grasped tightly by the six legs of a serpent who then sinks his fangs into the spirit's face. Gradually the two shapes become indistinguishable; then that which was the serpent becomes the shade, and the shade is the serpent.

While this is going on, an evil, black little reptile bites the second of the spirits. Smoke issues from both the mouth of the serpent and the wound of the shade, though the shade seems to take no notice of its wound. As the two jets of smoke meet, the legs of the spirit grow together, while the tail of the serpent divides; the skin of the snake softens, that of the shade grows scaly. The monstrous changes continue until the former spirit runs hissing away as a serpent, and the former serpent speaks in the shape of a man.

Dante's pen fails him, his eyes are clouded and his mind numbed, but he recognizes the third spirit, the only one unchanged, as that of Puccio Sciancato.

Commentary

The canto of the thieves begins with a long-drawn image which is couched in obscure phrasing. In the original it is a carefully contrived relief from the scenes Dante has just witnessed and a pause before viewing further torments. It is followed by a humorous passage describing Dante as he clambers with great difficulty up the stony bank of the chasm and trots breathless behind his master, talking to keep up the pretense. This is a very human Dante, poking a little fun at his stodgy self, and proves an effective contrast in style.

The obscene gesture of the thief startles Dante, and the poet's words concerning Pistoia are a curse rather than a lament. Fucci's cynical self-portrait, drawn with a sort of proud satisfaction, dwells on the baseness of his conduct, his origin, and his city. His shame is not born of repentance but rather of resentment and anger at being surprised in such a place and condemned to that horrible metamorphosis. He seeks revenge against Dante and utters the dark prophecy of the triumph of the Blacks only in the cruel hope of hurting the poet.

The transformations of the spirits and the serpents are described at length with terrifying vividness, but not with the tone used in telling about the demons of the fifth bolgia. Watching in horrified fascination, Dante seems to be recalling an evil nightmare, and words fail him at the end — an effective literary device that he will use again. The fifth spirit runs off unchanged, but we may easily guess that he will be next in the succession of dreadful transformations by which men are made beasts, and beasts, men.

CANTOS 26-27

Summary

Dante bitterly addresses his native city, whose fame has spread not only over the earth but also throughout Hell because of the actions of her citizens. He prophesies disaster in the future, and since he knows it will happen eventually, he wishes for it to happen now; his knowledge weighs heavily upon him and he is powerless to stop the disaster.

The travelers are at the eighth chasm, that of the evil counselors, and Dante sees little flames as numerous as fireflies on a summer night. He looks so intently that he nearly falls off the bridge and saves himself by catching hold of the parapet. His guide tells him that each of these flames holds a spirit and that each spirit holds close the fire which torments him. Dante has already observed this and asks the name of the spirit with a divided flame.

Virgil says that this flame holds two spirits, those of Ulysses and of Diomede, who together planned the stratagem of the Trojan horse. They also suffer torment for separating Achilles from Deidamia, who died of a broken heart, and for stealing the statue of Pallas, which guarded the city of Troy. Dante is eager to speak with these two. Virgil is pleased but reminds Dante that, since these spirits speak the Greek language and Dante does not, it might be best for Virgil to talk with them.

Virgil speaks respectfully to the double flame, recalling his own poetry to them and asking if he might know how Ulysses died, and where. The greater part of the flame speaks, flickering with each word. This is the spirit of Ulysses the wanderer, and in comparable language Dante tells the story of his last voyage.

Ulysses had at long last returned home, but neither the love of his wife and son, nor the respect due his father, could conquer the wanderlust that was in him. Once again he sailed the open sea, in one ship with a few trusted companions. He saw all the strange sights of the Mediterranean — Spain, Morocco, Sardinia — and then, because he and his comrades were old and desired to see more before they rested on shore forever, they passed through the Pillars of Hercules and sailed south on the unknown ocean.

For five months they sailed, until they could see the stars of the south pole and the guiding stars of the north were not visible above the horizon. And then one day they saw a mountain, the highest they had ever seen, and a hurricane rose from the land. It struck their ship, and the ship went down, bow first, and the waters closed over them.

The flame becomes silent and is dismissed by Virgil. It is followed by another, which speaks in such confused tones that Dante compares it with the bellowings of a brass bull used as an instrument of torture and death.

Finally the spirit is able to control the flame and speak intelligibly. It asks courteously to speak and wishes to know if the travelers have come recently from his own Latian land. Is there now peace or war? it asks.

Virgil says that Dante is a Latian, and Dante speaks immediately, giving a long discourse on the past and present troubles of that unhappy land: Romagna is at present not at war; Ravenna and Cervia are under the same ruler (whose crest is an eagle); Forli, once victorious over the French, is now ruled by Sinibaldo degli Ordelaffi (whose coat of arms is a green lion); Montagna is ruled by the cruel Rimini, father and son, whose castle is Verucchio; the cities on the Lamone and the Santerno are governed by a lord who tries to support both factions; and, finally, Cesena on the Savio is misruled by its appointed leaders.

Catching his breath, Dante asks the name and story of this spirit. The flame answers that it will tell the truth, since none ever returned to earth from here to tell the story. He was a soldier; then, repenting of his evil ways, he became a brother of the order of St. Francis. He had been famous for his cunning while he was a soldier but sincerely repented and became a monk. Heaven was his goal, and this he would have gained, except that the pope (Boniface VIII), who was making war, not upon infidels but upon other Christians, asked him to devise a plan of cunning and deceit, absolving him of sin in advance, as it were.

The plan was successful, and the pope triumphed. Meanwhile, the monk died and St. Francis descended from Heaven to receive his soul, as he did with every brother of the order, but a demon claimed the spirit, which had fallen into sin and had not repented. Even the absolution of the pope could not save him, and he was sent by Minos to this chasm of evil counselors. The flame moves away, and Dante and his guide go to the bridge that crosses the ninth chasm, that of the sowers of discord.

Commentary

In the realm of the evil counselors, Dante meets the spirits of Ulysses and Diomede in the form of a double flame. Virgil charges them to speak, naming their obligation to him in a kind of conjuration, and Ulysses tells the tale of his last voyage.

Poetically, this is another of the high points of the *Inferno*. The story is apparently an invention by Dante and, while beautiful in itself, serves also to display Dante's increasing sureness of touch in the handling of his material. Ulysses seems to be speaking in his own words, not Dante's, in contrast with the story of Francesca, for example, which was told in Dante's own style. Read the rallying cry of Ulysses to his crew, beginning with "Consider your origin. . . ." Then compare this with any part of Francesca's speech and with the stanza of the cranes, and the difference will be obvious. Francesca and Dante speak with one voice, but the story of Ulysses is the compelling, unembellished yarn of an experienced and courageous sailor. Dante has brought this legendary figure to life to tell its final story, a story that captures the imagination, and Ulysses is a powerful creation of unusual stature and tragic dimension.

Note that the two spirits cannot depart until dismissed by Virgil — the conjuration is ended. Here again, Dante has violated his own concept of the spirits being judged by the standards of their times. The action of Ulysses and Diomede in advising the building of the Trojan horse was, to the Greeks, an acceptable and admirable strategy of war. It is *Dante* who considers it an act of treachery.

Dante speaks with another figure, Guido da Montefeltro, who arouses his sympathy, and its story, like that of Ulysses, is told simply but forcefully. This spirit is not aware that Dante is alive and thus could reveal its sin when he returns to eath (ll.61-66). Only in ignorance does he confess his treachery to Dante. This tale does not have the appeal of the other, but its construction and language are as sound. Dante places the noble figure of the great soldier and repentant friar in opposition to the protagonist, Boniface VIII, for whom Dante reserves his bitterest invective because the pope dares to wage war, not against the Saracens, but against the Christians themselves, and because he is the instrument of the spiritual damnation of one of the sons of the church.

Though Guido is suffering the torture of the flames, he can still speak of the sweetness of his native land, an effective contrast. Boniface VIII, the Black Cherubim with his irrefutable logic, and St. Francis descending for his brother in Christ, are unforgettable images.

CANTO 28

Summary

Dante warns of the horrors to come, more gruesome than even he can describe. This is the place of the sowers of discord and scandal, and the creators of schism within the church.

The first one Dante sees is Mahomet, disembowelled, who tells him that his son-in-law and successor, Ali, is in the same condition and that all the others are horribly mangled in some manner. As they circle the chasm the wounds heal, but when they complete the circle the wounds are renewed by a devil with a sword.

The shade asks Dante's identity, suggesting that perhaps he is trying to delay his punishment. Virgil replies that Dante is alive and is being guided through Hell so that he may know what it is like (and presumably avoid it). A large group of spirits has now gathered to listen. Mahomet bids Dante deliver a message to Fra Dolcino, leader of a schismatic sect within the church, warning him to supply his community with food so that the Novarese will not be victorious because of the winter snow.

Mahomet's place is taken by another mutilated spirit who recognizes Dante. He asks Dante to warn Messer Guido and Angiolello that they will be drowned at sea by the treachery of a one-eyed ruler, who will summon them to a parley. The shade mentions one who wishes he had never seen the land (Rimini) of this treacherous ruler, and Dante asks to see this spirit. It cannot speak, however, and the first shade tells Dante it is Curio, who urged Caesar to cross the Rubicon. For this, his tongue has been slit and he is mute.

Another spirit has had his hands cut off. This is Mosca (de' Lamberti), whose rash counsel was the beginning of the disastrous rivalry between the Guelphs and the Ghibellines in Florence. Dante bitterly wishes death to all of Mosca's kindred, and Mosca, pained by this comment, walks away.

Now Dante sees something which is beyond belief. A headless spirit comes toward them, but in his hand he carries the severed head and swings it like a lantern. When he reaches the bridge, he holds up the head so it can speak, and it identifies the shade as Bertrand de Born. With his evil scandal, he caused father and son to become enemies, and now his brain, inventor of the tales, is parted from his body.

Commentary

Dante, viewing the sowers of scandal and dissension, describes in vivid terms the tortures and the sins of the damned. He views Mohammed as a sinner whose religious beliefs led to discord and schism.

Though he has seen the sowers of religious discord, Dante reserves his bitterest comment for the man whose evil counsel started the quarrel in Florence between the Guelphs and the Ghibellines. This man is Mosca dei Lamberti, and his advice caused the initial feud between two Florentine families, the Donati and the Amidei. A man betrothed to one of the Amidei broke the engagement (which in those days was as binding as marriage) and became engaged to a Donati. Mosca's counsel to the Amidei was brief: "A thing done has an end" (do it and get it over), and the man was murdered. As a consequence the offended Donati, to whom he was now allied by betrothal, began the vendetta which brought so much sorrow to Florence. Dante's words "And death to thy kindred!" cut across the dismal air like a whip.

The punishment of Bertrand de Born, a Provençal poet of some note, escapes the grotesque because of Dante's poetic skill. The spirit carries its head like a lantern because it used vicious scandals to separate father from son, namely Henry II of England and his eldest son. Thus it was aptly punished by having its head separated from its body. Dante expresses his own mystification and the lament of the spirit briefly and lucidly.

CANTOS 29-30

Summary

The sight of the tortured shades of the ninth chasm compels Dante to stay and weep; Virgil reminds him that they have not stayed this long at any other chasm, and that since their time is short, they must be on their way. Dante tells his master, in morose tones, that if he knew why Dante was waiting, he would not wish to hurry on. Following Virgil, Dante continues his lament: he had been looking for one of his own kinsmen in the ninth circle.

Virgil replies that he had seen the spirit just under the bridge; it had shaken its finger threateningly at Dante, and the other shades had called it Geri del Bello. This had happened while Dante was talking with the other spirit. Dante replies sorrowfully that the murder of Geri del Bello has not been avenged by those who plotted with him, and therefore his spirit was angry and went away without speaking. Somewhat defiantly, Dante says he still feels sorry for this kinsman.

While they have been speaking, they have reached the bridge over the tenth and last chasm of the eighth circle, Malebolge. So loud are the wails and weeping that Dante puts his hands over his ears and thinks of the noise of the hospitals of Valdichiana, and of Maremma and Sardinia, during the unhealthful summer season. Ever the experienced soldier, the stench reminds him of rotting human limbs.

They move across the bridge to the lower bank of the chasm, where Dante can have a better view. This dark and stinking place is that of the falsifiers, and Dante finds the air stifling. The diseased shades are lying in heaps, and some are crawling about. Dante sees two sitting together, scratching vigorously at each other and pulling off scabs as one scales a fish.

Virgil asks if there are any Latians among them, and the shades, weeping, reply that they are Latians, but who is it who asks the question? Virgil replies that he is guiding one who lives through the paths of Hell. The shades stop their scratching, and Virgil tells Dante that he may talk with them if he wishes. Dante of course asks them their names and their stories.

The first one says that he is Arezzo and was burned at the request of Albert of Siena when he told Albert, as a joke (he says), that he could teach him to fly; Minos, who knows all things, condemned him to this tenth chasm, not for his lie but because he was an alchemist, another form of falsifying. Dante remarks on the vanity of the Sienese, which makes them gullible subjects for the falsifiers, and the second shade speaks out, naming other Sienese he knew in his lifetime who were still more vain.

This spirit then tells Dante to look closely at him and he will see the shade of Capocchio, also an alchemist and, he says with a touch of vanity, a good one.

Two spirits run through the darkness. One comes to Capocchio, sinks its teeth in his neck and drags him off. The spirit who had first spoken trembles and says this rabid shade is that of Gianni Schicchi. Dante asks who the other one is, and is told that this is Myrrha, who conceived an incestuous passion for her own father and went to his bed disguised. Schicchi had conspired to falsify a will, using a disguise, and in so doing had gained possession of a fine mare known as the Lady of the Troop.

These shades have all gone, and Dante looks around at others, seeing one so swollen out of shape with dropsy that he looks like a lute. He identifies himself as Master Adam, counterfeiter of the gold coin of Florence, and he begs for water. He is unable to move but he would willingly give up even the sight of water if the other conspirators in the counterfeiting plan were here with him.

Dante asks the names of two who lie nearby. They are identified as the wife of Potiphar, who falsely accused Joseph, and Sinon the Greek, who was taken prisoner and then persuaded his Trojan captors to bring the wooden horse inside the walls of the city. One of the shades, insulted by his words, strikes Master Adam in the belly, which sounds like a drum. Master Adam quickly strikes back, hitting the shade in the face. The two begin bickering and insulting each other, and Dante listens intently.

Virgil speaks to him sharply for (apparently) enjoying this verbal exchange, and Dante shows that he is very much ashamed. Virgil smiles and says that so much shame would expiate a greater sin and he only wanted Dante to stop listening because the wish to hear such talk is vulgar.

Commentary

The death of Dante's kinsman had not been avenged at the time Dante was writing his poem. Geri del Bello's death was avenged by his nephews nearly thirty years later, and it required intervention by others, and a formal reconciliation before the feud was ended. To better understand the meaning of this episode as presented by Dante, one must remember that private revenge was, in Dante's time, both a right protected by law and a duty for the kinsmen of the person offended.

Dante enters the realm of the falsifiers, the last round of Malebolge, to describe new horrors with continued clarity. By the use of homely metaphors — pan leaning against pan, bedbugs keeping the sleeper awake — he shows with real impact the terrible punishment of the sinners. The noise of the place simply adds to the torture.

Dante had the gift of describing vividly in a few words, and the stories of the spirits here are excellent examples of this gift. The nostalgic evocation of the cool brooks and green hills of Master Adam's homeland is pathetic, coming as it does from the mouth of the thirsty wretch. His desire for vengeance is highly effective because it is at once so tenacious, and so impotent. The angry exchange between Master Adam and Sinon the Greek is told in terse, clear language, and Dante displays an all-too-human curiosity in what they have to say.

CANTO 31

Summary

Dante and his master climb the bank of the chasm in semi-darkness. Dante hears a horn sounding, as loud as thunder, and certainly louder than the horn of Roland. He looks intently in the direction of the sound and sees what appears to be a number of towers; he asks what town this is.

Virgil says it is too dark for Dante to see the forms properly, and when they arrive at the place where these things are, he will find that his eyes have deceived him. Then taking Dante by the hand, he halts for a moment, saying that it will be better for him to explain now so that Dante will not be startled by what he sees. These are not towers but giants in the pit of Hell (the ninth circle). They are ranged around its bank and sunk to the navel in the bank of the pit.

The travelers come closer, and Dante sees more clearly but is also more frightened, for the giants encircle the pit like the turrets of a castle wall. He sees one of the giants at close range and says that Nature was wise to discontinue the creation of these monsters. There is a place for other creatures of great size, like elephants and whales, but not for these, who because of their powers of reason and their faculty for evil are far more dangerous to man.

The giant which Dante sees has a face as long as the pine of St. Peter's and his body is in proportion, so that the part of his body which shows — from the navel up — is taller than three Frieslanders (a people noted for their great height). Suddenly the great mouth roars gibberish at the two poets, and Virgil calls him stupid, telling him to use his horn to vent his rage — adding insult by pointing out to him that his horn is hanging around his neck.

Virgil tells Dante that this giant is Nimrod, builder of the Tower of Babel, and that speaking to him is useless, for he can no more understand than he can be understood. They approach a second giant, larger and more frightening than Nimrod; he is held with a chain that circles his body five times from the neck down—Dante wonders who was strong enough to do this—with his right arm behind him, his left in front.

This is Ephialtes, one of the giants who made war against the gods. Dante wishes to see Briareus, one of the warring Titans, but Virgil tells him that Briareus is far off and tied like Ephialtes, and they will see only Antaeus, who is not confined and will set them on the bottom of the pit. The chained giant shakes himself until Dante is afraid they will be struck dead; then he remembers that the giant's hands are bound.

They reach a cavern just as Antaeus emerges. Virgil greets him with a recital of the giant's might on earth: he had killed a thousand lions, and if he had joined his brothers against the gods, the giants might have won. Virgil asks him to set them down on the base of the pit (Cocytus), telling him that Dante can give him what he desires: fame on earth.

As Antaeus stoops to lift them, Dante is reminded of Carisenda, the leaning tower of Bologna; he also recalls that Antaeus nearly defeated Hercules in a wrestling match. Dante fears for his life, fervently wishing there had been another way to descend, but Antaeus sets them gently in the pit which holds Lucifer and Judas, and again stands straight as the mast of a ship.

Commentary

Through the gloom of Malebolge, Dante gets his first glimpse of the Titans and giants. Their introduction is a bold one; he hears a horn louder than that of Roland and seems to see towers in the distance. These resolve themselves into gigantic figures: Nimrod, legendary builder of the Tower of Babel (hence his meaningless jabbering); Ephialtes, one of the giants who warred against the gods of Olympus; and Antaeus, who is not bound because he did not attempt revolt against the gods. Dante asks to see Briareus, a Titan who, with his brother Otus, attempted to scale Olympus.

According to legend, Antaeus was the giant who accosted any passing stranger and wrestled him to the death. Since Antaeus drew his strength from the earth, he was invincible as long as he could touch ground. He was slain by Hercules, who lifted him off the ground until he weakened, then crushed him. Antaeus is condemned to Hell for his many murders. Virgil plays upon his vanity—for he was very proud of his prodigious strength—to have him transport the two poets down the chasm.

If Dante erred in the writing of this canto, it was in being too specific about the size of the giants. Their size could have been left to the imagination, but Dante gets out his figurative yardstick and tells us the face of the giant was as tall as the pine of St. Peter's—a pine cone of gilt bronze that originally was probably ten or eleven feet high. He closes with the images of Antaeus as a moving tower and as the tall mast of a ship.

CANTOS 32-33

Summary

This is Cocytus, the frozen pit of Hell, which almost defies description. To Dante, it requires the use of all the coarse language at his command, and describing it is no task for one who uses the language of the jester or the child. Dante invokes the Muses, asking their help in speaking the truth. Angrily he addresses the spirits confined here, saying that it would have been better if they had been born sheep or goats!

A voice from the first round, Caina, warns him not to walk on the heads of his condemned brothers, and looking down he sees a lake of ice as clear as water. In it are spirits sunk to the chin; their teeth chatter as they look down at the ice and they weep bitterly. Near Dante's feet are two who are close together, and Dante asks their names. The spirits weep until their tears freeze, binding them more closely. This does not prevent them from butting at one another, and a third spirit, with both ears frozen off, tells Dante they are brothers. He adds there is none in Cocytus more deserving of punishment than these two. And if Dante is a Tuscan, he says, he should know the speaker, Camicion de' Pazzi.

The two poets have almost reached the center of the lake, when Dante accidentally kicks the face of a spirit. It weeps and asks why Dante should add to its misery. Dante asks Virgil to wait, and as the shade continues its wailing, Dante indignantly asks how it dares to reproach others. The shade angrily asks who Dante is, that he can go through Antenora (this second division of the pit) hitting the shades. Dante replies that he is alive and will give fame to the shade if he can learn its name, but the shade wants no mention of his name on earth and tells Dante to go away and stop bothering him.

A real altercation has begun between these two: Dante grasps the spirit's hair, demanding that he give his name or lose his scalp. The spirit heatedly replies that he will lose every hair a thousand times before he will tell. Dante has in fact pulled out some tufts of hair, and the spirit is still wrangling, when another shade calls out the name Dante seeks — Bocca — and tells the spirit to be quiet.

Dante is satisfied and tells Bocca to speak no more, but Bocca is undaunted and replies to Dante by giving the names of other traitors confined in the ice of Antenora.

Dante sees two more spirits confined close together — so close, in fact, that one is feeding upon the head and neck of the other. Dante asks their names and what their offenses were on earth, so that he may tell their stories.

The first spirit replies: it will cause him much grief to tell his story, but if it exposes the traitor who is confined with him, he will do so gladly, though he weeps as he talks. He knows that Dante is a Florentine; Dante should recall Count Ugolino, who is speaking, and Archbishop Ruggieri, the other shade. Ugolino was captured and put to death by Ruggieri—this Dante already knows—but the manner of his death was so cruel that the world should know the tragic story.

Ugolino had been in prison for several months, when he had a dream of the future. When he woke, he heard his four sons (actually two were grandsons), who were imprisoned with him, asking for food. At the time when their meal was usually brought, they heard the ominous sound of the door of the tower being nailed shut, and they were left to starve. One by one the sons died, and finally Ugolino, blind from hunger, died too.

Here his story ends, and once more the shade begins gnawing on the other's skull. Dante is both sad and indignant because of the tale Ugolino has told. It is true that Ugolino had betrayed certain strongholds of Pisa and deserved to die, but his sons deserved no punishment, and certainly not of that kind.

The poets move on to a place where the spirits are confined in the ice with their faces upraised, which causes their tears to form pools over their eyes and freeze them shut.

Dante has, of course, felt the cold as they crossed the ice; now he seems to feel a wind blowing and asks his master where it comes from. Virgil says they will soon reach the place that is the source of the wind.

One of the shades cries out to Dante to remove the ice from his eyelids, and Dante replies that he will if the shade will tell its name (rashly adding that he will go to the bottom of the ice if he does not keep his promise). The spirit replies that it is Friar Alberigo and gives a cryptic allusion to the murder of his younger brother. Dante is surprised to find him already dead, and he replies that he does not know whether his body on earth is dead or not, but he forfeited his soul by the betrayal of his brother. Therefore it is confined to Ptolomaea, this third division of the pit of Hell, while a demon inhabits his body on earth.

Dante finds this difficult to believe, for the shade has mentioned Ser Branca d'Oria, who is confined just behind him, and Dante is sure d'Oria is still alive. The shade assures him that d'Oria's spirit has been here for many years and that in the circle of the Malebranche above (in the boiling pitch) the spirit of Michel Zanche, whom d'Oria treacherously murdered, had not yet arrived when the soul of d'Oria came here. A devil took the place of his soul, though d'Oria *seems* to be alive.

The shade then asks Dante to remove the frozen tears as he had promised—and Dante refuses, considering rudeness a grace in Hell. Dante lashes out at the Genoese, immoral and corrupt, wishing them gone from the face of the earth, for he has found the soul of one in Hell while the body still walks the earth.

Commentary

At a loss for words, Dante again calls upon the Muses to come to his aid. This is the pit of Hell — the very center of evil, the abyss of Satan — and Dante recognized that the noble art of poetry is not designed to describe the horrors of this dreadful abode. Poetry is not usually devoted to harsh and grating words; therefore, Dante invokes the aid of the Muses to help him describe horror in poetic terms.

There are four rounds in this circle of traitors: Caina, for those treacherous to kin; Antenora, for those treacherous to country; Ptolomea, for those who betrayed guests; and Judecca, for those who betrayed masters. Caina is named for Cain; Antenora for the Trojan Antenor, who is portrayed as an excellent character in the *Iliad,* but who, in the Middle Ages, was universally believed to have betrayed Troy to the Greeks. Ptolomea derives its name from Ptolomey, a captain of Jericho and son-in-law of Simon the high priest. Ptolomey arranged a banquet honoring Simon and his two sons, then treacherously murdered them while they were his guests. Judecca is, of course, named for Judas Iscariot.

All the sins of the upper circles have flowed into this abyss, yet the ice has a startling clarity. Dante must have experienced a harsh winter somewhere, to be able to give this final circle its still, dead, frozen atmosphere.

And in the midst of it, Dante has a typically Dantean argument. With furious temper he attacks one of the frozen spirits, simply for the satisfaction of knowing its name so he can tell its story on earth. The violent anger which inspires his behavior reveals Dante as a man of his times, accustomed to cruelty and barbarity. These spirits, as noted before, want to be forgotten on earth because of their vicious crimes, unlike those in the upper circles, who ask to be remembered.

The story is a tragic one and yet takes only a part of the canto, so swiftly does the action move. Dante does not deny Ugolino's sin, but laments that the count's sons and grandsons shared his terrible fate. He does not discuss whether or not Ugolino's crimes were great enough to deserve death, but with pitiless energy he protests against the injury suffered by innocence and invokes a just revenge upon the ferocious executioners.

Ugolino's feelings are described with masterly gradation: after the warning dream, anguish and fear fill his heart. Soon after, he hears the door of the tower being nailed shut. At the moment when his suspicion becomes certainty, the desperation which takes hold of him is so great that he is denied even the comfort of tears. The man becomes the immortal representation of despair. He longs for death to come and to free him from the torturing sight of his starving sons, but death is slow to come, and he still must undergo a long agony before his final release.

The story of Ugolino is perhaps one of the most shocking in all the poem. Dante asks what hatred, what rage justifies such a horrible and bestial act, promising that if he hears the story he will right the wrong on earth. Thus Dante avoids emphasizing the crime of Ugolino and emphasizes, instead, Ugolino as a victim.

Here, in the pit reserved for traitors, we encounter Dante's intellectual concept of man become beast. In general this bottom part of Hell is the place where man has lost all of the qualities which ever distinguished him as being man. Every aspect of the inner essence of man has been frozen out of him. Ultimately Lucifer himself, at the very bottom of Hell, is nothing but a giant mass of matter, totally devoid of any intellect.

Two of the greatest characters in the *Inferno*, Francesca and Ugolino, are found at the beginning and at the end. There are many parallels that could be drawn. For example, Francesca was bound by love to Paolo at the beginning of Hell; and at the end we find another pair bound together, but Ugolino is bound to Ruggieri by hate. The first words Francesca spoke, "I will tell you my story as one who weeps and tells at the same time," have their counterpart in Ugolino's as he says "I will tell you but it renews the grief which is so desperate in me." Both characters recall the past with great reluctance and with grief. But the difference is also significant, for Francesca remembers a happy time which has brought her to her present damnation, while Ugolino remembers only the hatred and the horror which brought him here.

Ugolino's is the concept of retaliation. This is a masterful stroke on Dante's part, for in the pit of Hell, how else can he evoke pity for someone whose crime is so monstrous as Ugolino's? We note, therefore, that Ugolino is here in Hell as a traitor (which he is, having betrayed his party to Ruggieri), but also that he is here in the poem as the betrayed. Ugolino may be said to be both the victim of divine justice and also the instrument of it, in that he also punishes his betrayor, Ruggieri.

As Ugolino tells his story, we wonder how a man can hate so violently, then we realize that the hatred is so violent because he had loved with such great intensity; that his grief is so desperate because his love was so great; and that no amount of vengeance can ever satisfy his hatred because of all he has suffered.

There are two other striking passages. The first tells of a soul leaving the body after a foul betrayal has been enacted; with the spirit gone, the body still lives — or exists, for Dante describes it as only eating, sleeping, and wearing clothes. Dante violates his own concept of condemnation and repentance for the sake of a vivid poetic image. Even a murderer may repent, but Dante preferred the image of a soul seized at the instant of sinning and flung into Hell while the empty shell of its human form inhabits the earth.

The second is Dante's startling cruelty to Friar Alberigo. Dante fails to remove the ice from the Friar's eyelids, though he had promised to do so.

74

The friar has told Dante all he wished to know, and more, and Dante's only comment on his own callous act is that to be rude in Hell is a courtesy. Although he has previously shown sympathy and compassion, the increasing degradation of the sinners has forced upon him the conclusion that to feel anything but contempt for these base sinners is to go against the judgment of God. Allegorically, Dante's behavior suggests that treachery and brutality always evoke the responses of violence, for we have seen Dante respond with pity in the upper circles.

Dante closes the canto with an outburst against the city of Genoa, for he has found in Hell the spirit of one who still walks the streets of Genoa. Dante probably suspected that this spirit was not the only one of its kind in Hell.

CANTO 34

Summary

This is the source and the end of all evil, the abode of Satan. Virgil quotes in Latin the beginning of a hymn—The banners of the king go forth—and adds, ironically, *inferni:* the king of Hell. Dante peers ahead and sees a dim shape like a windmill in a mist. The wind is so cold he takes shelter behind his master. At his feet, completely covered with the clear ice, are the spirits of other traitors.

Dante and Virgil have come to a place where they can see Satan (Dis) clearly. Dante stands dazed and shaken in the presence of this hideous being and can only attempt to describe him.

Dis is frozen up to his breast in the ice of Cocytus, and so great is his size that one of his arms seems to be larger than the giants they have just passed. Dante is horrified to see that Dis has three faces: a red one in the middle, a black one on the left, and a yellow one on the right. Below each face is a pair of huge wings in continuous motion, and from them comes the wind which freezes Cocytus. Dis weeps with all six eyes, and from his mouths comes a bloody froth, for he is chewing the worst of traitors. In the red mouth is Judas Iscariot, who is also being clawed by Satan's talons; the black mouth tortures Brutus, and the yellow, Cassius.

Abruptly, Virgil says they must leave, and taking Dante upon his back, he waits until Satan's wings are extended backward, then begins the perilous climb down Satan's hairy side. They descend between Satan's body and the ice until they reach a point where Virgil turns completely around, with his head where his feet had been. Dante thinks they are returning to Hell, and when his guide, after great exertion, lifts him onto a rocky ledge, Dante is startled to see Satan's legs upright in a dismal cave.

Virgil orders Dante to his feet: it is very late, and there is a long, hard road ahead. Dante stands bewildered in this dark cavern. Where are they?

and where is the ice of Hell? Above all, how does Satan come to be upside down in this place?

Virgil explains that, in climbing down Satan's side, they passed the center of the earth and are now beneath the southern hemisphere. Satan has not moved. He is still fixed in the place to which he fell from Heaven; the earth above his head closed again and hid itself beneath the sea, while under his feet it was pushed upward. There is a stream (Lethe) which runs down to this hidden place from the earth above. Dante begins his climb to the living earth, and looking up, sees the stars.

Commentary

Dante has reached the center of the earth, and the climax of the *Inferno:* Judecca, the abode of Satan. Appropriately, Dante has reserved the worst fate in Hell for the traitors to church and empire, and they are in the grasp of the arch-traitor, Satan. This is an image of Satan that is scarcely expected. This is not Lucifer, son of the morning, as in the book of Isaiah; nor is he a fallen angel, nor the prince of darkness. Dante calls him the emperor of the dolorous realm, but the repellent figure with three heads scarcely has the majesty of a ruler.

But perhaps Dante had seen Satan as he really was: ugly, repulsive, abhorrent, the origin of all sin immobilized as a captive in the product of sin, as all the spirits of Hell are. Dante summed it all up in the sentence beginning "If he was once as beautiful as he is ugly now. . . ."

It is characteristic of Dante that he carefully develops parallels in the various sections of the book. The view of Satan at the climax of *Inferno* is matched by the vision of God in *Paradiso,* and the triple nature of Satan, symbolized by his three faces, is a parody of the trinity.

The rest is anticlimax. The poets make a hurried exit, scrambling down Satan's side. A few questions are answered, and the long, laborious climb begins. Only at the last does the magic return, when the poets step out onto the solid earth and for a brief moment look up at the stars.

LIST OF CHARACTERS

The number following each name refers to the canto in which the character *first* appears.

Achilles (12). One of the heroes of the Trojan War.
Adam, Master (30). Falsified the gold coin of Florence.
Alberigo, Friar (33). A Jovial Friar, who had his brother and nephew murdered.

Aldobrandi, Tegghiaio (16). A Florentine Guelph and one of the men Dante asked Ciacco about (Canto 6).

Amidei family (28). Florentines; one of the two feuding families (the other was the Donati) who caused the split between the Guelphs and the Ghibellines.

Anastasius, Pope (11). Called a heretic by Dante, who may have confused him with the Emperor Anastasius.

Annas (23). Father-in-law of Caiaphas, and a member of the Council which sentenced Jesus to death.

Antaeus (31). Giant slain by Hercules.

Arezzo (29). An alchemist, burned at the stake. He had told Albert of Siena that he could teach him to fly.

Argenti, Filippo (8). Florentine, and apparently a bitter enemy of Dante's.

Asdente (20). Soothsayer and prophet from Parma.

Attila (12). Chief of the Huns, called the "Scourge of God."

Barbariccia (22). A demon, leader of the Malebranche.

Beatrice (2). The inspiration for Dante's work, she entreats Virgil, on behalf of the Virgin Mary, to save Dante.

Bertrand de Born (28). One of the most famous of the troubadours of the twelfth century.

Bocca degli Abati (32). Traitor of Florence, and partly responsible for the defeat of the Guelphs at Montaperti.

Bonatti, Guido (20). Astrologer.

Boniface VIII, Pope (27). Bitter enemy of Dante's.

Branco d'Oria (33). Murdered his father-in-law, Michel Zanche.

Briareus (31). A giant who plotted against the gods of Olympus.

Brunetto Latini (15). Distinguished scholar; adviser and friend to Dante.

Brutus (34). One of the conspirators in the murder of Julius Caesar.

Caccianemico, Venedico (18). Guelph of Bologna. Arranged the seduction of his own sister, Ghisola.

Cacus (25). A monster mistakenly called a centaur by Dante.

Caiaphas (23). High priest who influenced the Council to assent to the crucifixion of Jesus.

Calchas (20). Greek soothsayer who allegedly foretold the day of sailing of the Greek fleet from Aulis to Troy.

Camicion de' Pazzi (32). Murdered one of his kinsmen.

Capaneus (14). One of the Seven against Thebes; defied Zeus to stop him from conquering Thebes and was killed by a thunderbolt.

Cappochio (29). An alchemist, probably from Siena. His name means "blockhead."

Cassius (34). Roman general; conspired with Brutus to murder Julius Caesar.

Catalano, Friar (23). *Podestá* of Florence.

Cavalcanti, Cavalcante dei (10). Father of Guido dei Cavalcanti.

Cavalcanti, Guido dei (10). Poet and close friend of Dante's.

Celestine V, Pope (3). Resigned the papal throne after only five months in office, making way for Boniface VIII.

Cerberus (6). The three-headed hound; in mythology, guardian of the gates of Hell.

Charon (3). Ferryman of the river Acheron in Hell.

Chiron (12). A centaur, legendary tutor of the Greek heroes.

Ciacco (6). A notorious glutton; his name means "the hog."

Ciriatto (22). One of the Malebranche; he has tusks like a boar.

Cleopatra (5). Queen of Egypt, mistress of Caesar and of Mark Antony.

Curio (28). Advised Caesar to cross the Rubicon.

Dante (1). Central figure in the *Inferno*.

Deidamia (26). Died of grief when she was abandoned by her lover, Achilles.

Dido (5). Queen of Carthage; killed herself on a funeral pyre when her lover, Aeneas, sailed away.

Diomede (26). Companion of Ulysses in the Trojan War.

Dolcino, Fra (28). Leader of a schismatic Christian sect.

Donati family (28). With the Amidei, originators of the split between the Guelphs and the Ghibellines.

Ephialtes (31). A giant who plotted with his brother Otus against the gods of Olympus.

Erichtho (9). Sorceress who conjured Virgil's spirit and sent him on his first journey through Hell.

Eurypylus (20). A Greek soothsayer, possibly associated with Calchas.

Fallen Angels (8). Oppose Virgil and Dante at the City of Dis as they opposed Jesus at the entrance of Hell.

Farinata degli Uberti (10). A prominent Ghibelline leader who defeated Florence, but averted her destruction.

Francesca da Rimini (5). Wife of Giancotto da Rimini, and lover of his brother Paolo.

Francis of Assisi, Saint (27). Founder of the Franciscan Order.

Frederick II, Emperor (10). Attempted to unite Italy and Sicily, but was defeated by the papacy.

Furies (9). Mythological figures of vengeance.

Geri del Bello (29). Cousin to Dante.

Geryon (17). A monster who represents fraud.

Gianciotto da Rimini (5). Husband of Francesca, and brother of Paolo; murdered both.

Gianni Schicchi (30). Aided Simone Donati in falsifying a will.

Gomita, Friar (22). A Sardinian, he was hanged for abusing the privileges of public office.

Grafficane (22). One of the Malebranche, part of the escort for Dante and Virgil.

Griffolino d'Arezzo (29). An alchemist, he was burned at the stake.

Guerra, Guido (16). A Florentine praised by Rusticucci for his courage and intelligence.

Harpies (13). In mythology, birds with the faces of women, who personify the winds.

Heavenly Messenger (9). Sent to force the admittance of Dante and Virgil to the City of Dis.

Helen (5). Wife of Menelaus, she was kidnaped by Paris, prince of Troy, thereby causing the Trojan War.

Homer (4). Great epic poet of Greece, author of the *Iliad* and the *Odyssey*. According to legend, Homer was blind.

Horace (4). One of the greatest of the Latin poets.

Interminei, Alessio (18). A Florentine, notorious for his flattery.

Jason (18). Leader of the Argonauts in their quest for the Golden Fleece.

Judas Iscariot (34). One of the twelve disciples, he betrayed Jesus for thirty pieces of silver.

Leopard (1). Symbol of incontinence.

Lion (1). Symbol of malice.

Lucan (4). A great Roman poet, he conspired against Nero and killed himself when the plot was discovered.

Lucia, Saint (2). Messenger of the Virgin Mary to Beatrice.

Mahomet; Mohammed (28). Founder of the Islamic religion.

Malebranche (21). Demons who guard and punish the barrators. The name means "evil-claws."

Malecoda (21). One of the Malebranche; his name means "evil-tail."

Manto (20). A sorceress, by legend responsible for the founding of the city of Mantua, Virgil's birthplace.

Medusa (9). One of the Gorgons. The sight of her snake-covered head turned men to stone.

Minos (5). One of the semi-legendary kings of Crete.

Minotaur (12). A monster with the body of a man and the head of a bull. Confined in the Labyrinth on Crete, he was slain by Theseus.

Montefeltro, Guido da (27). Military leader; later joined the Order of Franciscans.

Mosca de' Lamberti (28). A Florentine nobleman who advised the murder which started the feud of the Donati and the Amidei.

Myrrha (30). Princess of Cyprus, who conceived an incestuous passion for her father.

Nessus (12). One of the centaurs, killed in the battle at the wedding feast of Hercules.

Nichoals III, Pope (19). Successor to Pope John XXI; accused of simony by Dante and others.

Nimrod (31). "Mighty hunter before the Lord" (Gen. 10: 9), named as a giant by Dante.

79

Old Man of Crete (14). An allegorical figure based upon the Book of Daniel, and on Ovid's *Metamorphoses*.

Otus (31). A giant who, with his brother Ephialtes, plotted to scale Mount Olympus in defiance of the gods.

Ovid (4). Roman poet, whose best known work is the *Metamorphoses*.

Paolo da Rimini (5). Lover of Francesca, his brother's wife.

Phlegyas (8). Ferryman of the river Styx in Hell.

Pholus (12). One of the centaurs.

Plutus (7). God of riches. Dante may have confused him with Pluto, god of the underworld.

Potiphar's Wife (30). Falsely accused Joseph of attempting to seduce her (Gen. 39). Her name is not known.

Puccio Sciancato (25). Florentine, called a thief by Dante.

Rubicante (22). One of the Malebranche assigned to escort Dante and Virgil.

Ruggieri degli Ubaldini, Archbishop (33). Responsible for the death by starvation of Ugolino and his sons and grandsons.

Rusticucci, Jacopo (16). Wealthy Florentine statesman. His shrewish wife is said to have driven him to homosexual practices.

Satan (34). Also called Beelzebub, Lucifer, and Dis, he is the "Emperor of the Dolorous Realm."

Scala, Can Grande della (1). Dante's friend and protector in exile.

Scott, Michael (20). Scottish magician, often called a "wizard."

She-wolf (1). Symbol of bestiality or fraud.

Sinon the Greek (30). Accused of treachery during the Trojan War.

Socrates (4). One of the greatest of the Greek philosophers, he was condemned to die by drinking hemlock and met his death calmly.

Thais (18). A courtesan who flattered her lover excessively.

Theseus (12). King of Athens, slayer of the Minotaur, and one of the great lovers in Greek legend.

Ubaldini, Ottaviano degli (10). A cardinal of the church, he was overjoyed at the victory of the Ghibellines at Montaperti.

Ugolino della Gherardesca, Count (33). After much treachery on his part, Ugolino was imprisoned by Ruggieri, and consequently starved to death.

Ulysses (26). Legendary hero of Homer's *Odyssey*.

Vanni Fucci (24). Thief from Pistoia, who shocks Dante with his obscenity.

Vigne, Pier delle (13). Minister to Frederick II. He was imprisoned by Frederick (perhaps unjustly), and committed suicide.

Virgil (1). Dante's guide through Hell.

Virgin Mary (2). Alarmed at Dante's wandering, she commands Virgil, through Beatrice, to escort him through Hell.

Vitaliano (17). A usurer, the only one mentioned by name by Dante, but whose identity is not clear.

Zanche, Michel (22). Governor of Logordo in Sardinia. He was murdered by his son-in-law, Branco d'Oria.

80

REVIEW QUESTIONS AND ESSAY TOPICS

1. The punishment of sinners is usually by analogy or by antithesis. Discuss one canto where Dante follows his plan closely. Where does he depart from it?
2. Punishment is accorded the condemned by the standards of their own society. Where in the *Inferno* does Dante fail to follow this basic concept of Hell?
3. Would you arrange the sins and punishments of Hell in a different order? If so, how? Should some of the sins have punishments other than those Dante has given them?
4. There is a notable absence of women — particularly Dante's contemporaries — in the *Inferno*. How do you account for this?
5. Dante seems particularly attracted to certain types of characters and emphasizes the episodes concerning them. Who are some of these characters? Why, in your opinion, was Dante drawn to them?
6. Virgil is extremely important to the *Inferno,* both symbolically and in his own person. Explain this importance.
7. Mythology plays a large part in the *Inferno*. Compare the mythological characters and places as used by Dante with the same characters and places as understood today.
8. The *Divine Comedy* was written in *terza rima*. Describe this rhyme scheme. Has it been used successfully in English poetry, other than in translations?

SELECTED BIBLIOGRAPHY

ANDERSON, WILLIAM. *Dante the Maker*. London: Routledge and Kegan Paul, 1980.

AUERBACH, ERICH. *Dante, Poet of the Secular World*. Trans. R. Manheim. Chicago: University of Chicago Press, 1961.

BAROLINI, TEODOLINDA. "Why Did Dante Write the *Commedia*? or The Vision Thing." *Dante Studies* 111 (1993): 1–8.

BERGIN, THOMAS G. *Dante*. New York: Orion Press, 1965.

_____, ed. *From Time to Eternity: Essays on Dante's* Divine Comedy. New Haven, Connecticut: Yale University Press, 1967.

_____. *Perspectives on* The Divine Comedy. Bloomington: Indiana University Press, 1970.

BLOOM, HAROLD, ed. *Dante's* The Divine Comedy. New York: Chelsea House, 1987.

BRANDEIS, IRMA. *Discussions of* The Divine Comedy. Boston: Heath, 1961.

_____, ed. *The Ladder of Vision: A Study of Dante's* Comedy. Garden City, New York: Doubleday, 1960.

CAMBON, GLAUCO. *Dante's Craft: Studies in Language and Style*. Minneapolis: University of Minnesota Press, 1969.

CASSELL, ANTHONY K. *Dante's Fearful Art of Justice*. Toronto: University of Toronto Press, 1984.

CHIARENZA, MARGUERITE MILLS. The Divine Comedy: *Tracing God's Art*. Boston: Twayne, 1989.

CHUBB, THOMAS CALDECOT. *Dante and His World*. Boston: Little, Brown, 1967.

CLEMENTS, ROBERT J., ed. *American Critical Essays on* The Divine Comedy. New York: New York University Press, 1967.

DAVIS, CHARLES TILL. *Dante's Italy and Other Essays*. Philadelphia: University of Pennsylvania Press, 1984.

DEMARAY, JOHN G. *The Invention of Dante's* Commedia. New Haven, Connecticut: Yale University Press, 1974.

DURLING, ROBERT M. "Deceit and Digestion in the Belly of Hell." *Allegory and Representation*. Ed. Stephen Jay Greenblatt. Baltimore: Johns Hopkins University Press, 1981. 61–93.

FARNELL, STEWART. *The Political Ideas of* The Divine Comedy. *An Introduction*. Lanham, Maryland: University Press of America, 1985.

FARRANTE, JOAN M. "Why Did Dante Write the *Comedy*?" *Dante Studies* 111 (1993): 9–18.

FERGUSSON, FRANCIS. *Dante*. New York: Macmillan, 1966.

FOSTER, KENELM. *The Two Dantes and Other Studies*. Berkeley: University of California Press, 1977.

FOWLIE, WALLACE. *A Reading of Dante's* Inferno. Chicago: University of Chicago Press, 1981.

FRECCERO, JOHN. *Dante: The Poetics of Conversion.* Cambridge, Massachusetts: Harvard University Press, 1986.

_____. "Infernal Irony: The Gates of Hell." *Modern Language Notes* 99 (1984): 769–86.

_____. "Introduction to *Inferno.*" *The Cambridge Companion to Dante.* Ed. Rachel Jacoff. New York: Cambridge University Press, 1993. 172–91.

FREINKEL, LISA. "*Inferno* and the Poetics of Usura." *Modern Language Notes* 107 (1992): 1–17.

GIAMATTI, A. B., ed. *Dante in America: The First Two Centuries.* Medieval and Renaissance Texts and Studies 23. Binghamton, New York: Medieval and Renaissance Texts and Studies, 1983.

HARRISON, ROBERT POGUE. "Comedy and Modernity: Dante's Hell." *Modern Language Notes* 102 (1987): 1043–61.

HAYWOOD, ERIC. *Dante Readings.* Dublin, Ireland: Irish Academic Press, 1987.

HOLLANDER, ROBERT. *Allegory in Dante's* Commedia. Princeton, New York: Princeton University Press, 1969.

_____. "Why Did Dante Write the *Comedy?*" *Dante Studies* 111 (1993): 19–25.

HOLMES, GEORGE. *Dante.* Oxford: Oxford University Press, 1980.

KIRKPATRICK, ROBIN. *Dante:* The Divine Comedy. New York: Cambridge University Press, 1987.

KLEINER, JOHN. "Mismapping the Underworld." *Dante Studies* 107 (1989): 1–31.

LIMENTANI, U., ed. *The Mind of Dante.* New York: Cambridge University Press, 1965.

MASCIANDARO, FRANCO. *Dante as Dramatist: The Myth of the Earthly Paradise and Tragic Vision in the* Divine Comedy. Philadelphia: University of Pennsylvania Press, 1991.

MASON, H. A. "A Journey through Hell: Dante's *Inferno* Re-Visited." *The Cambridge Quarterly* 21 (1992): 222–42.

MUSA, MARK, ed. *Essays on Dante*. Bloomington: Indiana University Press, 1965.

NASSAR, EUGENE PAUL. *Illustrations to Dante's* Inferno. Rutherford, New Jersey: Fairleigh Dickinson University Press, 1994.

NOLAN, DAVID, ed. *Dante Soundings. Eight Literary and Historical Essays*. Dublin, Ireland: Irish Academic Press, 1981.

PAYTON, RODNEY J. *A Modern Reader's Guide to Dante's* Inferno. New York: Peter Lang, 1992.

PEQUIGNEY, JOSEPH. "Sodomy in Dante's *Inferno* and *Purgatorio*." *Representations* 36 (1991): 22–42.

QUINONES, RICARDO J. *Dante Alighieri*. Boston: Twayne, 1979.

REICHARDT, PAUL F. "Dante's Dogs: Imagery of Hound and Hunt in the *Inferno*." *Kentucky Philological Review* 4 (1989): 27–33.

SINGLETON, CHARLES S. Commentary. *Inferno*. By Dante. Bollingen Series. Princeton, New Jersey: Princeton University Press, 1970.

SLADE, CAROLE, ed. *Approaches to Teaching Dante's* Divine Comedy. New York: Modern Language Association of America, 1982.

SMITH, HERBERT W. *The Greatness of Dante Alighieri*. Bath, England: Bath University Press, 1973.

WILLIAMS, CHARLES. *The Figure of Beatrice*. New York: Octagon Books, 1972.